How?

More experiments for the young scientist

Dave Prochnow and
Kathy Prochnow

Chelsea House Publishers

Philadelphia

Disclaimer

This book deals with subjects, materials, and procedures that can be hazardous to your health. Use extreme caution when performing this book's experiments. Do not attempt to perform any of these experiments unless you fully comprehend all of the materials' associated handling precautions. If you lack this information, consult with a science teacher or another adult.

Although every possible safeguard has been employed in ensuring the accuracy of this book's information, neither the authors nor Chelsea House Publishers can be held liable for damages or injuries that could result from the application, misinterpretation, and/or misapplication of the materials and procedures that are discussed in this book.

This Chelsea House Edition with Permission of the McGraw-Hill Companies.

Product or brand names used in this book may be trade names or trademarks. Where we believe that there may be proprietary claims to such trade names or trademarks, the name has been used with an initial capital or it has been capitalized in the style used by the name claimant. Regardless of the capitalization used, all such names have been used in an editorial manner without any intent to convey endorsement of or other affiliation with the name claimant. Neither the author nor the publisher intends to express any judgment as to the validity or legal status of any such proprietary claims.

Library of Congress Cataloging-in-Publication Data

Prochnow, Dave.
    How? : experiments for the young scientist /
Dave Prochnow & Kathy Prochnow.
     p. cm.
    Originally published: Blue Ridge Summit, Pa. : TAB Books, 1993.
    Includes index.
    Summary: Presents forty-three experiments in such areas as
structural engineering, astronomy, chemistry, and meteorology.
    ISBN 0-7910-4846-2 (hardcover)
    1. Science—Experiments—Juvenile literature. 2. Engineering-
-Experiments—Juvenile literature. 3. Science—Miscellanea-
-Juvenile literature. 4. Engineering—Miscellanea—Juvenile
literature. [1. Experiments.] I. Prochnow, Kathy. II. Title.
[DNLM: 1. Science—Experiments]
Q164.P84 1997
507'.8—dc21
                                      97-24043
                                          CIP
                                          AC

Contents

PART 4
THE YOUNG METEOROLOGIST

PART 5
THE YOUNG BIOLOGIST

PART 6
THE YOUNG PHYSICIST

Introduction

You are about to take a journey into the world of science. As you might remember from your previous journey, this scientific encounter will be unlike any you have ever had. You won't have to take any tests or quizzes, and you won't have to learn any complex formulas. It is impossible to make a mistake.

You begin your excursion as a scientist. And, as different scientists study different disciplines, so will you explore the world of questions from various points of view: as an engineer, astronomer, chemist, meteorologist, biologist, and physicist.

As you perform the experiments, make observations, and record results, you will be examining the following scientific disciplines:

structural engineering
architecture
cartography
computer science
interior design
logic
botany
entomology
ecology
electronics
geology
paleontology
astronomy
chemistry
mathematics
meteorology
physics

How to use this book   This book is divided into six parts: The Young Engineer, The Young Astronomer, The Young Chemist, The Young Meteorologist, The Young Biologist, and The Young Physicist. In each part, you will find a series of hands-on experiments that answer such complicated questions as, "How do emulsions work?", "How does fog form?", and "How does a crayfish breathe?"

Each experiment is a self-contained study; therefore, you can perform any experiment at any time. You don't have to read the chapters through in order, and you don't have to do every experiment. We suggest that you begin with the subjects that interest you most and that you work with an adult who enjoys exploring the scientific world as much as you do.

When you look at the experiments, you'll notice that each has five sections:

How?   Each experiment begins with a *how* question. The question is the reason for conducting the experiment.

Materials   This is a list of the tools and supplies that you will need to perform the experiment.

Procedure   Written as step-by-step directions, this section tells you how to do the experiment.

Results   This is a brief description of the expected reactions, conclusions, and results of the experiment.

Further studies   This section has more information—and sometimes more experiments—for a better understanding of the *how* questions.

The intended benefit of this book is that when you have successfully completed an experiment, you will have an answer. Each of these answers, however, will be only as good as the scientist who obtains them. In the laboratory, good scientists keep good records of all their experiments—and so should you.

As you do each experiment, write down three things: what you did, what you saw, and what you think happened. These are your procedures, observations, and conclusions. A good place for your records is right here in this book; in this way, a book of questions becomes a personalized book of answers to those questions. Of course, if the book doesn't belong to you or if you don't wish to write in it, another solution is to use a spiral-bound notebook.

Before starting any experiment in this book, be sure that you and an adult—your parent or teacher—read the experiment together. Some of the experiments call for using scissors, a hot iron, burning candles, harsh chemicals, and other dangerous items. Learn how to use these tools safely.

Discuss with your parents or teachers whether you can do the experiment independently or if you must have assistance. Your parents or teachers might prefer that you do all the experiments with them.

The following symbols are used throughout the book as a guide to what you might be able to do by yourself and what you should do with adult supervision.

Materials or tools used in this experiment could be dangerous and, if they are used irresponsibly, exhibit the potential for injury to the young scientist. Work with an adult, and learn how to handle sharp tools and combustible or toxic materials.

 Wear protective gloves that are flame-retardant and heat-resistant. Protect surfaces beneath hot materials (with towels or heat pads).

 Wear protective safety goggles to shield your eyes from shattering glass or other hazards that could damage your eyes.

 Burning candles, canned heat, or other sources of open flames are used in this experiment. Work with an adult. Do not wear loose clothing, and be sure to tie your hair back. Never leave a flame unattended, and be sure to extinguish it properly. Protect surfaces beneath open flames.

 The stove or oven is used in this experiment. Work with an adult, and keep other small children away from boiling water and hot burners.

 Electricity is used in this experiment. Work with an adult. Plug in and un-plug appliances carefully.

Chemicals, fertilizers, soap, plants, leaves, moldy bread or moldy fruits are used in this experiment. Do not taste—or eat—these materials. They can burn your mouth or make you very sick.

Part I
The Young Engineer

Engineering is subdivided into several different disciplines or branches of science. Even though each discipline relates to a specialized engineering problem, it must still answer the need for combining art with science, which is the foundation of engineering. The various engineering disciplines include civil engineering, structural engineering, electrical engineering, mechanical engineering, traffic engineering, chemical engineering, and agricultural engineering. One underlying factor present in each of these engineering disciplines is that they serve to make life more comfortable for human beings. Likewise, this comfort level is achieved through the unique application of art and science.

How does a helicopter fly?

Materials   ❐ Several sheets of typing paper
                ❐ Scissors

Procedure   1. Cut and fold the typing paper as shown in the helicopter plan (FIG. 1-1).
                2. Your helicopter is now ready for vertical flight.
                3. Make several flights with this design.

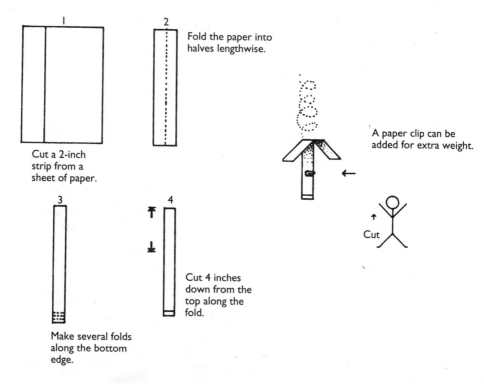

Cut a 2-inch strip from a sheet of paper.

Fold the paper into halves lengthwise.

A paper clip can be added for extra weight.

Cut

Make several folds along the bottom edge.

Cut 4 inches down from the top along the fold.

1-1   Paper helicopter design.

Results The helicopter is a specialized airplane. While an airplane is able to fly only vertically, a helicopter is able to fly in both vertical and horizontal directions. This unique flight ability comes from combining *lift* and *thrust* into a single location: the rotating blade on the top of a helicopter. Actually, this blade, or *main rotor,* is a wing that is moving at the speed of a propeller.

Because of their unique method of movement, helicopters are also known as *rotary-winged airplanes.* Helicopters that need increased stability and control have another, smaller rotor on their tail. This tail rotor spins perpendicular to the main rotor and acts like a rudder-control surface on a "normal" airplane.

Further studies Changes in the shape of a main rotor's blade angle are used to control a helicopter in flight. This angle is called the *pitch* of the rotor's blades. By altering the pitch of the rotor, the helicopter can be made to climb, dive, turn, and hover. A helicopter is hovering when it remains at a fixed, stationary altitude (FIG. 1-2). Try to change the pitch of your helicopter's rotor. Can you control your helicopter through pitch changes?

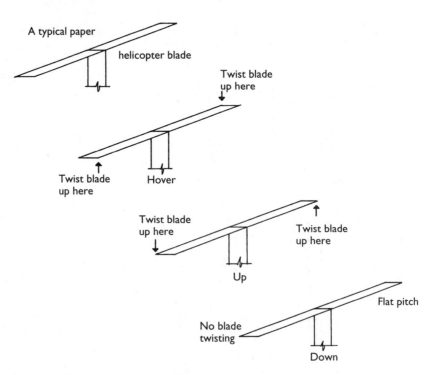

1-2 Procedure for adjusting blade pitch on a helicopter.

Did you know?   ○ It was Leonardo da Vinci who began working with helicopter designs in 1500. His work, however, failed to reach the actual testing stage. It wasn't until 1907—when two French brothers, Louis and Jacques Bréquet, made a two-rotor helicopter—that the first successful helicopter flight was made.

○ The first successful direct-lift helicopter was constructed by Vought-Sikorsky Aircraft, Stratford, Connecticut, in November of 1939.

How does a propeller work?

Materials
- ❏ 8½-x-11-inch piece of cardboard (tablet back)
- ❏ Rubber band
- ❏ Two common pins
- ❏ Cellophane tape
- ❏ Pliers

Procedure
1. Cut and fold the cardboard into the test-stand shape shown in FIG. 2-1. Use cellophane tape to secure the final assembly.
2. Cut a propeller from the cardboard, similar to the one found in FIG. 2-2.
3. Carefully poke one of the pins through the propeller's center, and tape it to the propeller.
4. Insert the other pin through the back of the test stand, and tape the pinhead to the test stand.
5. Bend the pointed end of both pins into a "J-hook" with the pliers.
6. Hold the propeller against the front of the test stand with its hook going through the provided opening.
7. Slip the rubber band over the propeller's hook, and loop the other end over the test stand's hook.
8. Your test stand is now ready for experiments with thrust.
9. Turn the propeller with your finger to wind the rubber band until it is tight and twisted.
10. Release your finger.

Results   A propeller is also known as an *air screw*. As the engine turns the propeller, it pulls the airplane through the air. This action is similar to the way a screw is pulled into wood as a screwdriver turns it.

   Actually, the shape of a propeller is responsible for its ability to produce forward thrust. A propeller is shaped like the wing of an air-

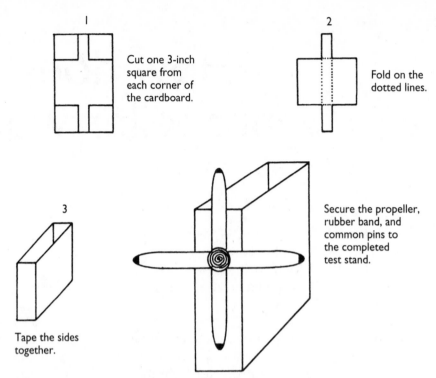

2-1 Procedure for building a propeller test stand.

1 Cut one 3-inch square from each corner of the cardboard.

2 Fold on the dotted lines.

3 Tape the sides together.

Secure the propeller, rubber band, and common pins to the completed test stand.

plane. This means that a rotating propeller generates greater air pressure behind the propeller, making it move forward. As the propeller moves forward, it pulls the airplane through the air. The pulling action of this propeller gave it the name *tractor propeller.*

Further studies Certain airplane designs use propellers that are mounted on the tail behind the wings. The original Wright 1903 Flyer, built by Orville and Wilbur Wright, used this design. These propellers push the airplane through the air and are called *pusher propellers.* Try to make your propeller test stand into a pusher propeller. There is more to making an effective pusher propeller than just twisting the rubber band the opposite direction, however. Does the pusher propeller generate enough thrust to push the test stand?

Did you know? ○ The first air stewardess was Ellen Church. She flew her first flight May 15, 1930 between San Francisco, California and Cheyenne, Wyoming.

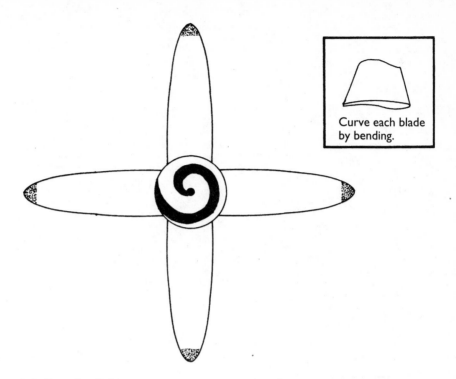

Curve each blade by bending.

2-2 Propeller design.

How does an airplane's jet engine work?

Materials
- ❏ Drinking straw
- ❏ String
- ❏ Balloon
- ❏ Cellophane tape

Procedure
1. Run the string through the drinking straw.
2. Tie the string between two chairs that are at least 10 feet apart.
3. Inflate the balloon with your breath.
4. Hold the end of the balloon so that none of the air escapes.
5. Tape the balloon to the straw with several pieces of cellophane tape.
6. Move the balloon along the string until the end you are holding is against one of the chairs.
7. Release the balloon (FIG. 3-1).

Results

Changes in air pressure make a jet engine move forward. This is the same action/reaction that moved the balloon down the string when it was released. The action in a jet engine is the exhaust. The reaction is the jet engine moving forward. In 1687, Sir Isaac Newton stated this law of motion as "to every action there is an equal and opposite reaction."

One important ingredient in making a jet engine work is oxygen. Oxygen is needed to burn the fuel that gives the jet engine its energy. The great amount of energy or thrust that is produced by the jet engine far exceeds the output from a conventional propeller/piston engine combination. A German aircraft company, Ernst Heinkel A. G., flew the first jet-powered airplane in 1939.

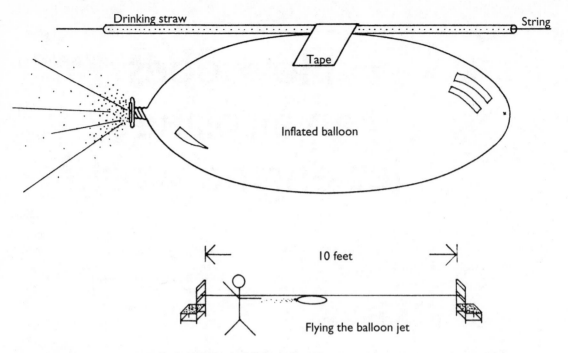

3-1 Procedure for building a balloon jet.

Further studies You can make a number of design improvements that can increase the efficiency of a jet engine. Can you think of any changes to your jet balloon that will increase the distance it can travel? Experiment with different tailpipe exhaust shapes. Will your new shape make the jet balloon travel 20 feet?

Did you know? ◯ The first civilian to fly faster than the speed of sound was Herbert Henry Hoover on March 10, 1948. His plane was the rocket-powered Bell X-1.

Experiment 4

How do space rockets work?

Materials
- ❑ Safety goggles
- ❑ Four Alka-Seltzer tablets
- ❑ Water (about 4 Tbs.)
- ❑ Pop bottle
- ❑ Cork
- ❑ Knife

Procedure
1. Thoroughly rinse out the pop bottle.
2. Make sure that the cork fits the pop bottle. If the cork is too big for the pop bottle, carefully shave the cork with a knife until it fits snugly in the bottle opening.
3. Put on safety goggles!
4. Pour 4 tablespoons of water into the pop bottle.
5. Add 4 Alka-Seltzer tablets to the bottle.
6. Quickly place the cork in the bottle and set the bottle upright in the middle of the table (FIG. 4-1).

CAUTION: This reaction causes a mild explosion. Don't point the bottle at anyone.

Results A rocket operates on the same action-reaction principle found in jet engines. The only difference between the rocket and a jet engine is that the rocket does not require an external source of oxygen to work properly.

There are two ways that a rocket can carry its own oxygen. First, the oxygen can be held in a separate fuel tank. This type of rocket is called a *liquid-fuel rocket*. All of the major NASA (National Aeronautics and Space Administration) rockets use this technique. The second way a rocket can carry its own oxygen is when it is already mixed with the

4-1 Results from the pop bottle rocket.

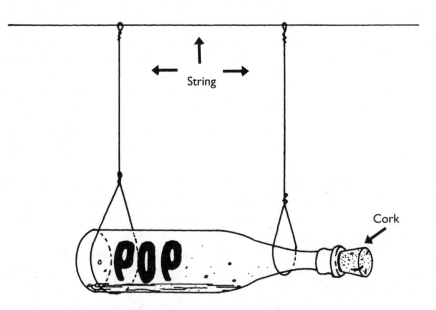

4-2 Enhanced procedures for building pop bottle rocket.

fuel. This rocket is called a *solid-fuel rocket*. Skyrockets used on the 4th of July use this method of propulsion.

Occasionally, a spacecraft will use both types of rockets at the same time. For example, the NASA space shuttle has a liquid-fuel main engine and two solid-fuel booster rockets. This combination gives the shuttle greater thrust for lifting big payloads into space.

Your rocket motor works on a chemical reaction that generates a large amount of carbon dioxide (CO_2) gas. The expanding CO_2 gas pops the cork out of the bottle.

Further studies In order to see the full impact of the CO_2 action-reaction, make the following modification to your rocket motor. Tie a length of string between two chairs. Securely tie two 24-inch strings to the top and bottom of the bottle. Enough string should remain so the string on the bottle can be tied to the one on the chairs (FIG. 4-2). Repeat the fueling procedure with 4 tablespoons of water, followed by 4 Alka-Seltzer tablets. Cork the bottle and let it hang from the strings. What happened when the cork popped?

Did you know ○ Robert H. Goddard filed the first liquid-fueled rocket engine patent on July 14, 1914.

Experiment 5

How do airplane wings work?

Materials ❐ One 8½-x–11-inch piece lightweight cardboard
❐ Cellophane tape
❐ Pencil
❐ Electric fan

Procedure 1. Cut, fold, and tape the cardboard into the wing shape shown (FIG. 5-1).
2. Slip the wing shape over the pencil and tape it on.
 3. Turn on the electric fan.
4. Hold the wing shape in front of the fan.
5. Evaluate the effect of the airflow over the wing shape.

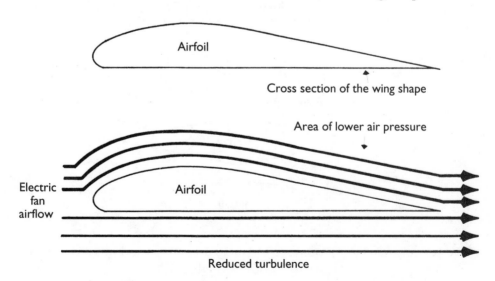

Airfoil

Cross section of the wing shape

Area of lower air pressure

Electric
fan
airflow

Airfoil

Reduced turbulence

5-1 Airflow around an airfoil.

17

Results The air from the electric fan simulates the air moving around the wing as the airplane is flying. A successful wing design must be longer along its top surface than along its bottom surface to make it *aerodynamic* This increased length causes a decrease in pressure to form on the top surface; as a result, the greater pressure created on the bottom pushes the wing up. Pushing the wing up gives lift to the airplane and helps it to fly.

Modern wind tunnels are large enough to hold full-sized airplanes. Very rarely are large airplanes tested, however. Usually, small models of the full-sized airplane are tested before the actual construction of the new design is begun. Today's wind tunnel is able to move air at various speeds under different air pressure and air temperature settings. All of these factors help give an accurate picture of the actual flight characteristics of the real airplane before its has ever been test flown.

Further studies Different wing shapes provide different amounts of lift. Make various original wing shapes and test them in your wind tunnel (for some suggested shapes, see FIG. 5-2). During your tests, use a flat piece of cardboard to alter the flow of air over the top and bottom surfaces. Place this piece of cardboard between the fan and the wing shape. Does this affect the lift produced by the wing shape?

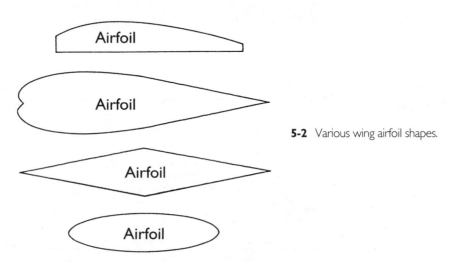

5-2 Various wing airfoil shapes.

Did you know? ○ Automobile manufacturers use wind tunnels to measure the car's ability to "slide" through air.

How does the binary numbering system work?

Materials
- ❐ Heavy paper (8-x-8-inch)
- ❐ Scissors
- ❐ Ruler
- ❐ Pen

Procedure

1. Cut the heavy paper into the binary calculator shape shown, which is 5 inches by 8 inches (FIG. 6-1).

 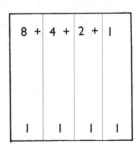 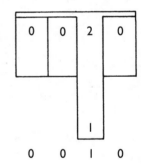

6-1 Procedures for building a binary calculator.

2. Holding the paper with the long edge at the top, label the calculator with the numbers 8, 4, 2, and 1 centered every two inches. Write a + in between each of these numbers as shown in the illustration.
3. Make three parallel, 2-inch-deep cuts in the bottom of the calculator (one every 2 inches).
4. Fold each of these strips along the top of its cut.
5. Write a 1 on each of these strips.

6. On the back of each strip write a 0.

7. Your binary calculator is now ready for use.

Results The binary numbering system has only two digits: 0 and 1. This is different from our decimal number system, which has 10 digits (0, 1, 2, 3, 4, 5, 6, 7, 8, and 9). Computers are able to make use of the binary numbering system by assigning either an OFF or ON electrical condition to the 0 and 1, respectively. Therefore, all computer operations are controlled through the turning on and off of electrical current.

These two events are even further simplified by special computer flip-flop circuits that change between an ON or an OFF condition by flipping back and forth between the two. Based on this explanation, the leading question is, "If computers only use 0 and 1 for mathematical functions, how can all of the possible number combinations be computed?" Actually, the computer combines 0s and 1s into strings that represent the decimal number equivalents. Your binary calculator is able to show you the binary numbers for the decimal values 0 to 15.

In order to use your calculator, you must fold up or down the required bottom strip. After these folds are completed, either a 0 or a 1 will be visible on each strip. If a 0 is visible, then you do nothing. If a 1 is visible, however, then the decimal number above the one is added to any other decimal numbers that have 1s visible. For example, the binary number 0010 is equal to the decimal value 2. In this case, a 1 is visible below the number 2. Therefore, only that number is added to the final value. Some other examples include:

$$1001=8+1=9$$
$$0011=2+1=3$$
$$1101=8+4+1=13.$$

Further studies This binary calculator is handy for small numbers, but what about converting larger numbers? A binary calculator for 8-position binary numbers could lead to some complicated addition. A better solution is to write a simple program that makes a computer do all of the math for you. Can you write a simple binary calculator program? Does your program handle all binary numbers? Can your program solve the binary number 11100110?

One possible solution to the problem is given in the program in FIG. 6-2. This program is written in a plain version of BASIC (Beginners'

```
5      REM BINARY CALCULATOR PROGRAM
10     INPUT "HOW MANY DIGITS ",A
20     B=0:C=0:D=0:Z=0:PRINT "ENTER YOUR";A;"–DIGIT BINARY NUMBER:
INPUT QB$
30     D=A–1
40     FOR B=1 TO A
50          IF MID$(QB$,B,1)="1" THEN LET C=2^D:Z=Z+C:D=D–1
60          IF MID$(QB$,B,1)="0" THEN LET C=0:Z=Z+C:D=D–1
70     NEXT B
80     PRINT QB$;"=";Z
100    INPUT "DO ANOTHER: Y OR N? ",X$
110    IF X$="Y" THEN GOTO 10
120    IF X$="N" THEN END
130    IF X$<>"Y" OR X$<>"N" THEN GOTO 100
```

6-2 BASIC binary calculator program.

All-Purpose Symbolic Instruction Code). It should work on Apple II, Commodore 64, and IBM personal computers. Macintosh, Amiga, and Atari ST owners will have to make only minor adjustments to the program for it to work. Just type this program into your computer and enter the RUN command. You will now be able to find the decimal values for any binary number.

Did you know?   O Herman Hollerith formed the Tabulating Machine Company around 1890. This has since become the computer giant IBM.

How do computers solve problems?

Materials ❐ Paper
❐ Pencil

Procedure 1. Write an explanation of how to solve addition problems. This explanation should be thorough enough so that anyone reading your description could answer any addition problem.
2. Set up your final written explanation as a flowchart for solving addition problems.
3. Trade your explanations with another person who has written the same type of flowchart.
4. Use a clean sheet of paper and try to solve the following addition problems. Perform only the instructions that are written on the flowchart. If you have a question that the flowchart doesn't answer, stop at that point.

$$3 + 2 \quad\quad =$$
$$334 + 55437756 =$$
$$57 + 993 \quad\quad =$$

Results The secret to a successful flow chart is that it must perform small steps in a logical order. At every point where a possible question can arise, you should have several answer possibilities. This will give the person reading your explanation a choice. By breaking the task—in this case, addition—into small steps with numerous choices, you can more easily monitor the progress of someone using your flowchart.

This same basic procedure is used when programming a computer (FIG. 7-1).

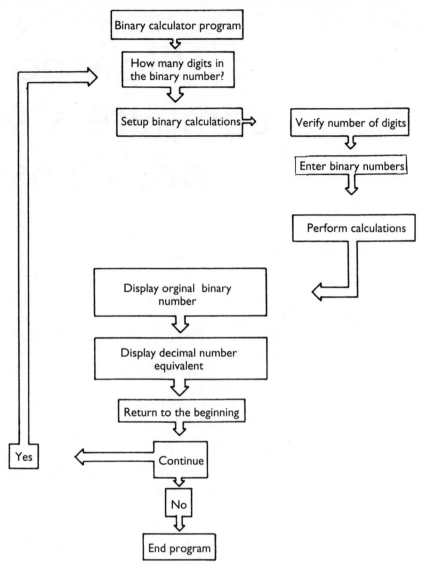

7-1 Flowchart for BASIC binary calculator program.

Further studies   Now that you have a flowchart for addition, can you convert it into a real computer program? Is your program able to solve any addition problem? Even the best written program can lead to areas where the computer will not know what to do. How can you prevent these errors from occurring? Errors can also rise from incorrect human input. What are some possible methods for safeguarding your program from faulty input?

One final important quality for any program is that it must be easy to use. In other words, the human operator must be able to run the program without difficulty. How did you write your program so that it is easy to use?

Did you know?   ◯ The development of high-level programming languages began with Assembler, which was only one step above machine language.

How do circuits cause lights to flash?

Materials
- ☐ 3909 IC (Radio Shack Part No. 276-1705)
- ☐ 220 µF electrolytic capacitor (Radio Shack Part No. 272-1029)
- ☐ Red LED (Radio Shack Pad No. 276-01)
- ☐ Battery holder (Radio Shack Part No. 270-402)
- ☐ One C battery
- ☐ Wire
- ☐ Breadboard

Procedure
1. Plug the 3909 IC into the breadboard as shown (FIGS. 8-1 and 8-2).
2. Insert the 220 µF capacitor in its correct location. Be sure to observe the proper orientation of the capacitor (notice which wire is the ground side).

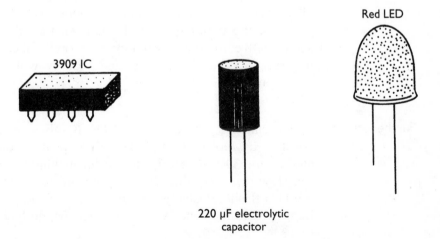

Red LED

3909 IC

220 µF electrolytic
capacitor

8-1 Materials needed for LED flasher.

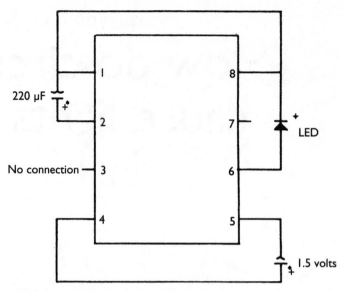

8-2 Schematic diagram for LED flasher.

 3. Plug the LED into the breadboard.
4. Connect the battery holder to the breadboard.
5. Add the necessary wire for completing the circuit.
6. Place the battery in the battery holder.
7. Your LED is now flashing.

Results The 3909 IC is an oscillator that causes LEDs to oscillate. Connecting the capacitor to the IC creates voltage surges that are applied to the LED. By varying the value of the capacitor the frequency of the oscillation can be changed. The frequency of the oscillation is the speed of the blinking on and off. Even though the circuit is constantly active, there is a very low drain on the life of the battery from this simple circuit. In fact, your C battery will run this circuit for about one year.

Further studies The oscillating nature of the 3909 IC also enables it to drive a speaker. By replacing the LED with a speaker, tones can be generated by the 3909 IC. Study FIG. 8-3 for making the 3909 tone generator. How does the tone that is produced relate to the frequency of the LED flashing? Change the resistance of the potentiometer. What happened to the tone? Why does this change have an effect on the tone?

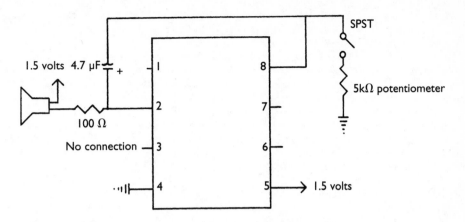

8-3 Schematic diagram for 3909 tone generator.

Did you know? ⭕ The first electric sign was built by Edison General Electric Company in 1892 and contained 1,457 Edison bulbs.

Experiment 9

How do digital displays work?

Materials
- ❏ 555 IC (Radio Shack Part No. 276-1723)
- ❏ 7490 IC (Radio Shack Part No. 276-1808)
- ❏ 7447 IC (Radio Shack Part No. 276-1805)
- ❏ 1 kΩ resistor (Radio Shack Part No. 271-1321)
- ❏ Seven 330 Ω resistors (Radio Shack Part No. 271-1315)
- ❏ 1 MΩ potentiometer (Radio Shack Part No. 271-211)
- ❏ 10 µF electrolytic capacitor (Radio Shack Part No. 272-1013)
- ❏ Switch (Radio Shack Part No. 275-645)
- ❏ LED digit (Radio Shack Part No. 276-053)
- ❏ battery holder (Radio Shack Part No. 270-391)
- ❏ Four AA batteries
- ❏ Wire
- ❏ Breadboard

Procedure
1. Plug the 555 IC, 7490 IC, and 7447 IC into the breadboard as shown (FIGS. 9-1 and 9-2).

2. Plug the eight resistors into their respective breadboard locations.
3. Add the potentiometer to the circuit.
4. Insert the capacitor into the breadboard at its indicated position.
5. Connect the battery holder to the breadboard.
6. Plug the switch into its breadboard site.
7. Wire the remaining circuit connections.
8. Add batteries to the battery holder.
9. Your digital timer is now ready to use as an egg timer.

Results Your digital timer must be calibrated before it can be used. The circuit is calibrated by turning the potentiometer until the proper time is seen on the LED digit. To calibrate this circuit:

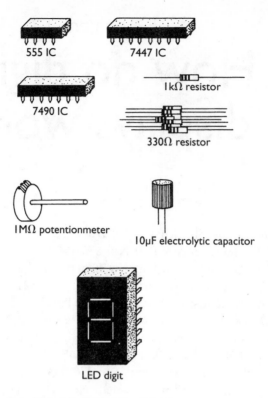

Materials needed for digital timer.

1. Turn on the power switch.
2. Watch the numbers change on the LED digit.
3. Adjust the potentiometer for a one-minute interval between each number change on the LED digit. This adjustment is made by turning the potentiometer.
4. Your digital timer is now calibrated as a minute timer. You can also calibrate the circuit as a second timer.

NOTE: Your digital timer is capable of counting only from 0 to 9 minutes (or 0 to 9 seconds).

Further studies You can make your digital timer count from 0 to 99 by making a slight modification to this circuit. Can you design a circuit based on your experimental timer that can count from 0 to 99? The only requirement for such a circuit would be to duplicate the circuit and connect the two pieces together. How would you connect these timing circuits together? Figure 9-3 offers one possible solution to this problem.

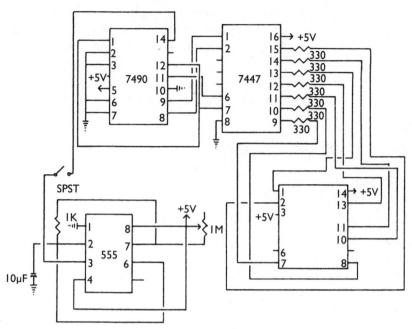

9-2 Schematic diagram for digital timer.

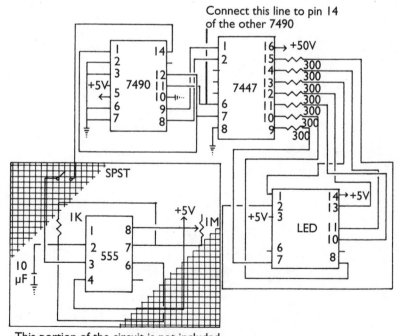

Connect this line to pin 14 of the other 7490

This portion of the circuit is not included on the second 7490/7447/LED digit construction.

9-3 Schematic diagram for 2-digit digital timer.

These circuits offer a beginning for constructing an hourly clock. How would you design such a circuit? Each digit on a clock resets at a different value. For example, the hour's tens position cycles at 1, while the minute's tens position cycles at 5. How would you make your clock reset at the proper times? Can this be done with the parts contained in this experiment?

Did you know? ○ The digital computer was invented by Howard Aiken in 1944.

Experiment 10

How can we get energy from the sun?

Materials   ❏ Three silicon solar cells (Radio Shack Part No. 276-124)
           ❏ One dc motor (Radio Shack Part No. 273-223)
           ❏ Cardboard

Procedure   1. Cut the cardboard into a propeller shape (FIG. 10-1).
           2. Press this propeller onto the shaft of the dc motor.
   3. Connect the three solar cells into a series circuit (FIG. 10-2).
           4. Wire the motor to the solar cells.
           5. Place the solar cells in direct sunlight.

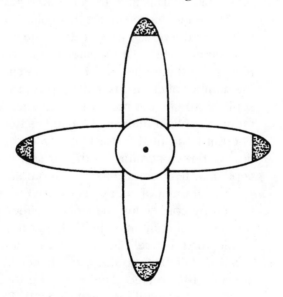

10-1 Propeller design for solar-powered motor.

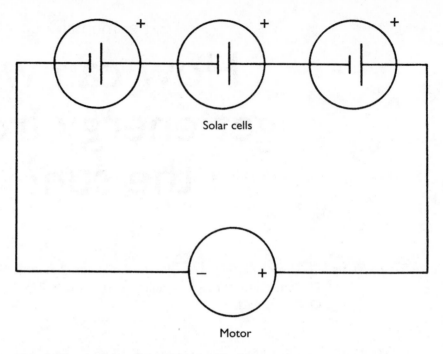

Solar cells

Motor

10-2 Schematic diagram for solar-powered motor.

Results These solar cells are made of a silicon semiconductor. They are able to convert photons from sunlight into electrons for energy. One of these solar cells is able to generate 0.42V in direct sunlight.

Three factors can affect this voltage output. First, the type of circuit using the power produced by the solar cell will drain the current at a variable rate. The greater the amount of circuit resistance, the higher the drain rate. Second, the intensity of the sunlight will vary the number of electrons that are produced. Basically, the stronger the sunlight, the higher the solar cell's energy level. The accepted maximum in sunlight intensity is stated as full sun at noon on a clear day. The third and final factor that affects the solar cell's energy production is the temperature of the air surrounding the solar cell. An accepted air temperature for maximum energy production is 76°F.

The amount of voltage generated by a group of solar cells can be altered by connecting the cells in either series or parallel circuits. A *series circuit* combines the voltage output of the solar cells. For example, the three cells in the experiment have a total voltage of 1.26V. A *parallel circuit,* on the other hand, increases the current without affecting the voltage. Therefore, the three solar cells in the experimental circuit would generate only 0.42V when connected in a parallel circuit.

Further studies Can solar cells be used to power the propeller test stand in Experiment 2? How many solar cells would be necessary for powering this circuit? How would you wire these solar cells together? In series? In parallel? Could a motor speed control be made from the circuit in this experiment? Can the speed of the motor be altered by varying the amount of sunlight that strikes the solar cells? Is this an efficient speed-control technique?

Experiment 11

How do remote controls work?

Materials
- ❏ Two LM324 ICs (Radio Shack Part No. 276-1711)
- ❏ Two IR LEDs (Radio Shack Part No. 276-142)
- ❏ MPS2222A Transistor (Radio Shack Part No. 276-2009)
- ❏ 4.7 µF electrolytic capacitor
- ❏ 10 µF electrolytic capacitor
- ❏ 0.1 µF capacitor
- ❏ Two 1 kΩ resistors
- ❏ Two 100 kΩ resistors
- ❏ 220 kΩ resistor
- ❏ Two 100 Ω resistors
- ❏ 1 MΩ potentiometer
- ❏ Dynamic microphone (Radio Shack Part No. 33-1054)
- ❏ Two battery snaps (Radio Shack Part No. 270-325)
- ❏ Two 9-volt batteries
- ❏ Wire
- ❏ Two breadboards
- ❏ Amplifier (Radio Shack Part No. 277-1008)

Procedure
1. Study FIG. 11-1, then wire the two circuits on separate breadboards. Use one breadboard for the IR transmitter and use the other breadboard for the IR receiver circuit.
2. Insert the 324 ICs into each breadboard.
3. Add the resistor and capacitors at their proper locations. Follow FIG. 11-2 for location instructions.
4. Insert the MPS2222A transistor in the transmitter breadboard.

5. Plug each of the IR LEDs into its proper breadboard location. Bend the LEDs so they are in a direct line with each other. The light produced by the transmitter IR LED must fall on the lens of the receiver's IR LED.

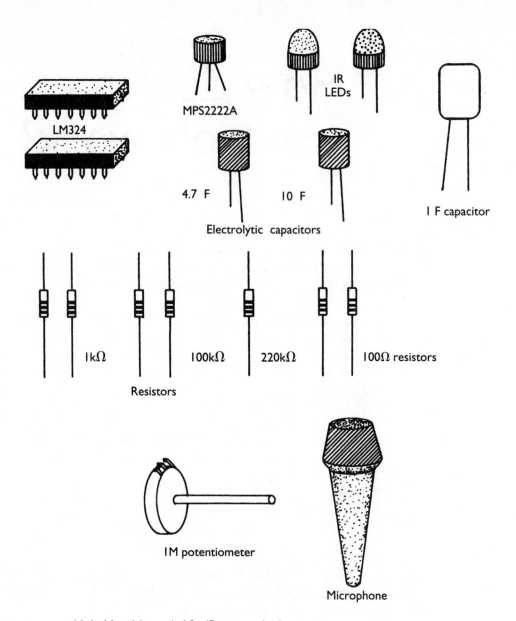

LM324

MPS2222A

IR
LEDs

1 F capacitor

4.7 F   10 F

Electrolytic capacitors

1kΩ   100kΩ   220kΩ   100Ω resistors

Resistors

1M potentiometer

Microphone

11-1 Materials needed for IR communications system.

6. Attach the potentiometer to the transmitter circuit.
7. Connect a battery snap to each of the IR circuits.
8. Attach the amplifier to the receiver circuit and attach the microphone to the transmitter.
9. Insert a battery in each circuit's battery snap.
10. The IR transmitter/receiver is now ready for use.

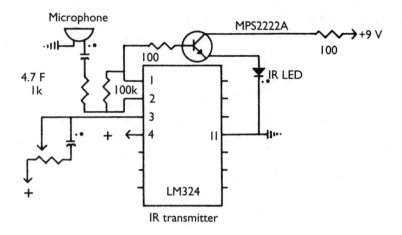

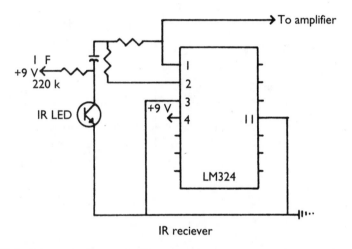

11-2 Schematic diagram for IR communications system.

Results You should make several tests of your circuit design before you attempt to use it operationally. Each of these tests is performed with the transmitter 6 inches away from the receiver. Make sure that the light beam from the transmitter IR LED is striking the receiver's IR LED. Now, plug a battery into each circuit and turn on the amplifier. Speak into the microphone. You should hear your voice in the amplifier. Adjust the volume control on the amplifier to increase output, and rotate the potentiometer on the transmitter to adjust the voice quality.

When you are satisfied with the operation of your circuits, move the units several feet apart. You can now speak into the transmitter and hear your voice in the receiver's amplifier. You can increase the distance between these two circuits if you dim the room's lighting and add a lens to each IR LED.

Further studies Your IR transmitter/receiver operates on the same principle used by remote-control television sets. In the case of these remote controls, a sign pattern is transmitted instead of a voice. The receiver then interprets this pattern and executes the programmed command. By removing the amplifier circuit and using a relay, a limited remote control system can be designed from these basic circuits. Can you build a remote control circuit based on your experiment IR transmitter/transceiver?

Another advanced project for use with this experiment is to build your own audio amplifier. The amplifier you build can then be used in place of the amplifier used in Step 8. A 386 IC is perfect for designing a low-cost amplifier. Figure 11-3 shows a simple method for building an audio amplifier with an LM386 IC.

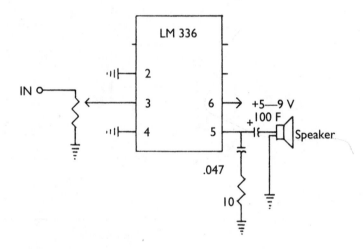

11-3 Schematic diagram for IR amplifier.

1. Insert the 386 IC as shown in the wiring diagram.
2. Plug in the resistors and capacitors at their proper locations.
3. Attach the power supply to the amplifier.
4. Connect an 8-ohm speaker to the amplifier outputs.
5. Wire the remaining pins of the 386 IC and connect the IR receiver circuit to the amplifier.
6. Your IR receiver is now ready to receive light communications. You can adjust the volume of the speaker's output by rotating the potentiometer that is connected to the 386 IC. The final circuit is operated exactly like the version that is described in Experiment 11.

Experiment 12

How do spiders spin webs?

Materials
- ❐ 10-x-10-inch piece of foam core board
- ❐ 10 yards of yarn
- ❐ 60 common pins
- ❐ Thimble
- ❐ Misting bottle

Procedure 1. Locate a spider web. (If no spider web is available, use FIG. 12-1 as your visual source.)

Dictyna spider

Featherlegged spider

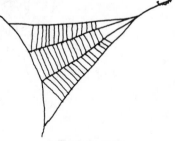

Triangle spider

12-1 Three types of spider webs.

43

2. Mist the spider web so that the complete design is visible.

3. Study the web. Locate the points where the web threads touch each other.

4. Push the pins into the board at all of these support points and all of these intersection points.

5. Wind the yarn around the pins in the same pattern as the web.

Results A spider's web is actually made from a liquid that is produced by a special spider organ called the *spinneret.* The average spider has several spinnerets located on its abdomen. When a spider touches its spinneret to an object, such as a leaf, a small drop of this liquid is produced. This liquid hardens as the spider pulls its abdomen away from the leaf. The result is the beginning of a web thread. By repeating this process several hundred times, the spider is able to make a complete web. This process is sometimes called *weaving* or *spinning* a web.

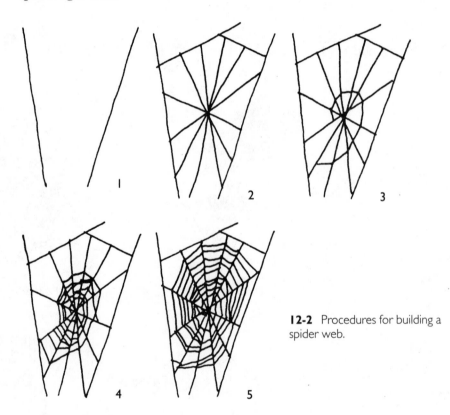

12-2 Procedures for building a spider web.

The average garden spider begins its web by building a framework that can hold the final web. After this framework is complete, the spider hangs from the center of the upper web frame and attaches shorter web pieces, which accumulate until the web is finished (FIG. 12-2). The spider then uses the completed web as a trap. Many of the web's threads are coated with a sticky substance that will hold any insect that comes into contact with them (FIG. 12-3). Once the web has trapped an insect, the spider will produce more liquid from its spinneret and encase the insect inside a pocket of webbing. Following a quick bite from the spider, the insect is then paralyzed and saved for subsequent consumption.

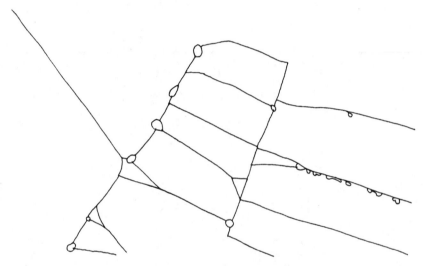

12-3 Spiders secrete a sticky substance onto their webs in order to ensnare other insects.

Further studies Different spiders have different methods for building webs. These different web-construction techniques usually result in webs with varied shapes. Several of the more common web shapes are orb, sheet, triangle, funnel, and blanket. See if you can locate an example of each of these webs. Can you duplicate these web shapes with your pins and yarn? How do the shapes affect the function of the web?

How do skyscrapers keep from falling?

Materials ☐ 50–75 hardbound books, each at least 1" thick

Procedure 1. Find a large open area of floor space.
2. Begin stacking the hardbound books on top of each other.
3. Continue to stack the books as high as you can.

Results *Skyscraper* is a term that came into usage in 1883. Although Louis Sullivan is credited with popularizing the skyscraper, William Le Baron Jenney actually designed the first skyscraper—the Home Insurance Building in Chicago. New York City, however, eventually became the "skyscraper capital of the world."

Those who designed and built the first skyscrapers were challenged by many of the same difficulties you faced during your stacking experiment. As the height of a structure increases, the weight on its base increases. This increased weight must be displaced; if the skyscraper's base is not enlarged, the entire building will become unstable. Engineers use complicated structural bracing to help counteract the enormous weight stress placed on a skyscraper's base. Frank Lloyd Wright, a famous architect, proposed a skyscraper that would be a mile tall. This design, which was not built, was scheduled for construction in Chicago.

Further studies As we have discussed, bracing is one method for increasing the height of a skyscraper. Can you think of a method for bracing your book stack? After you brace your base, add more books to the stack. Does the bracing allow you to add more books? How tall can you stack the books with this bracing? Let each book represent 50 feet in the overall height of a skyscraper. Can you place enough books together to build a scale model of Frank Lloyd Wright's one-mile-tall skyscraper?

You can play a game that combines your knowledge of skyscraper architecture with your knowledge of geography. Can you match the famous skyscraper with its city (FIG. 13-1)?

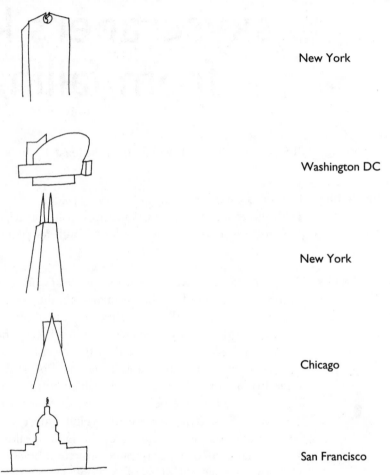

New York

Washington DC

New York

Chicago

San Francisco

13-1 Match the landmark skyscraper to the city in which it is located.

Did you know? ○ Cathedrals built in Europe use flying buttresses to help support the great weight of the structure.

How are maps constructed?

Materials
❏ Typing paper
❏ Pencil
❏ Ruler
❏ Protractor
❏ Tape measure
❏ Compass

Procedure
1. Locate an outdoor site, such as a park, a zoo, or a shopping mall.
2. Determine a point within this site. This point will be your destination.
3. Draw a detailed map of your site. Use the ruler, compass, protractor, and tape measure to make your map extremely detailed.
4. Clearly mark the destination on the map.
5. Exchange your map with a classmate. Have your friend walk to the destination that you have marked on your map, using only your map for instructions on locating the destination.
6. Find the destination that your friend has indicated on her or his map.

Results Every map should contain five points:

1. Name
2. Symbol key
3. Directions
4. Distance
5. Landmark features

A map's *name* is usually a descriptive term that labels the purpose of the map. For example, a state map will have a name that corresponds to the name of the state.

One problem with a map is that it is a two-dimensional representation of a three-dimensional feature. To help you visualize an area that is described by the map, special two-dimensional symbols are used to indicate three-dimensional objects. A *symbol key* labels the meaning of these two-dimensional symbols (FIG. 14-1).

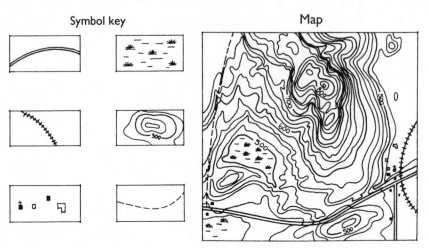

Symbol key   Map

14-1 Features of a contour map. Can you read this map with the symbol key?

Knowing the *direction* and *distance* between objects is vital in using a map. A simple arrow indicating a north compass heading is the standard means for showing a map's direction. Furthermore, a distance scale is used for converting a map distance (for example, 1 inch) into a true distance (such as 1 mile).

Finally, *landmark features* on a map give the map reader identifiable visual reference points. Some possible landmark features include a bridge, mountain range, or a famous historical building. Did the map that you made contain all five of these points?

Further studies Understanding and using a compass is important in any advanced map activity. The better the compass, the more accurately you will be able to read a map. A compass can be used for moving without a map, also. Use a compass to take a reading of an object in your room. If you are using an orienteering compass, do the following:

1. Point the compass base at the room object.
2. Line up the base's direction arrow with the object.
3. Now turn the compass dial until the magnetic needle is lined up with the north symbol (N).
4. Read your bearing from the index line. This is the directional heading you would need to take to move toward the object.

As a test of your compass handling ability, place 10 cards around a room. The cards should be numbered from 1 to 10. Place an X on the floor to mark the spot from which you will take all your readings. Now, take a bearing from card number 1. Write this compass value down on a piece of paper. Repeat this procedure with each numbered card. Have a friend duplicate this experiment. Are both of your compass readings the same?

If you have a large outdoor area, perform this experiment outside. In this case, travel to each of the numbered cards before you take a reading from the next one. Try to place the cards in hard-to-see places. Are you still able to locate each card by following the compass heading? If you get lost, just turn your compass around and follow the reverse heading back to your starting point.

Part 2
The Young Astronomer

Navigation, calendars, and clocks are all controlled by the actions of numerous astronomical bodies or objects. Another aspect of astronomy that is enjoyed by everyone is gazing at the nightly star patterns. Over one-half of these patterns or constellations were originally mapped by the ancient Greeks before the year 2 A.D., which is one reason the constellations have names taken from Greek mythology. Names like Hercules, Cassiopeia, and Perseus not only fill our literature, but our night skies, as well.

Experiment 15

How does the night sky change?

Materials ❏ Camera with an adjustable shutter speed
❏ Tripod
❏ Roll of Kodak Tri-X ISO 400 OR T-max ISO 3200 black-and-white film

Procedure 1. Load your camera with the film.
2. Try to find a location without any street lights, then fix the camera on the tripod.
3. Locate the North Star.
4. Point the camera at the North Star.
5. Open the camera's shutter and leave it open for 1 hour. Adjustable cameras have two shutter-speed settings for making this exposure. Use the T setting for a timed exposure, or use the B setting for manually holding the shutter open. Refer to your camera manual for the correct exposure technique with either of these shutter speeds.
6. Close the shutter after the hour's time.
7. Develop and print the film (FIG. 15-1).

Results Actually, this experiment is a slight modification of the intended results. Your final print only proves that the earth does indeed revolve around on its axis. In order to prove the real point of this experiment, that the earth revolves around the sun, it would require that the shutter be held open for 365 days, 6 hours, 9 minutes, and 9.54 seconds. Because of limitations in film sensitivity (and your time), this would be impossible.

Under real conditions, the constellations can be seen to move slowly to the west through the four seasons. This change can best be seen by looking due south on the fifteenth of each month at 9:00 P.M.

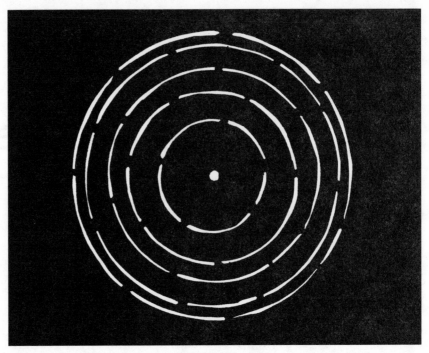

15-1 Simulated photograph of the North Star's rotation.

Over time, new constellations will appear from the east and move to the west. After one year, your view will return to the original constellation pattern that you began watching.

Further studies Photographing constellations is an intriguing hobby that requires a keen eye and tremendous patience. Two things are extremely important when taking pictures of constellations. First, use a good, solid tripod for holding your camera. Any camera movement during the actual exposure will give poor results. Second, use as short an exposure time as possible. If the exposure time is too long, what will happen? To take a constellation picture, fix the camera on the tripod and point it toward the desired star group. Next make the exposure. For good results, make sure that you experiment with various exposures (FIG. 15-2).

You can also produce constellations artificially through a series of apertures, light bulbs, and colored filters. A room or device that is used in this artificial projection of constellations is known as a *planetarium*. An inexpensive method for constructing your own planetarium is illustrated in FIG. 15-3. You can use almost any small box in

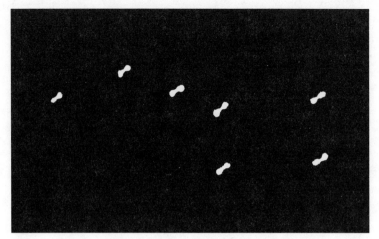

15-2 Simulated photograph of the Big Dipper constellation.

the construction of your planetarium, but empty cereal boxes make the best constellation projectors.

Did you know? ○ Johann Kepler published his *Laws Of Planetary Motion* about 100 years before Isaac Newton published his *Laws Of Motion*.

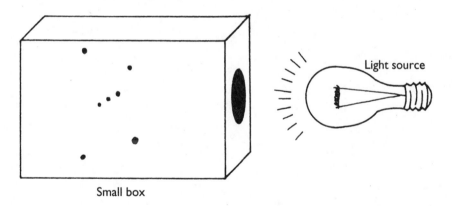

Small box

15-3 Procedure for building a constellation generator.

How were star patterns named?

Materials   ❏ Clear February night sky

Procedure   1. Go outside at night to a location where there is little influence from streetlights.
2. Face south at approximately 9:30 p.m.
3. Look at a point midway between the horizon and your zenith. (Your zenith is the point directly over the position where you are standing.)

Results   You are looking at the constellation of Orion (FIG. 16-1). In Greek mythology, Orion was the son of Poseidon. According to the legend, Orion was accidentally shot with an arrow by Artemis. Following Orion's death, Artemis placed him in the night sky as the constellation that you see.

Three well-known stars make up the shoulders and left knee of Orion. Bellatrix, the left shoulder of Orion, is a blue giant that is very young in the total age of the universe. The right shoulder of Orion is formed by Betelgeuse, which is a red giant star. Betelgeuse is an older star than Bellatrix. The last familiar star in the Orion constellation is the blue giant Rigel, located at the left knee of Orion. Actually, Rigel is two stars that are orbiting each other. This type of a star pattern is called a *binary system*.

Further studies   Go outside and look in the same general area where you located Orion. This time, however, do your observing on a clear September night. Can you spot Orion? What are the names of the other constellations that are in front of you? Near the southwest horizon there is a

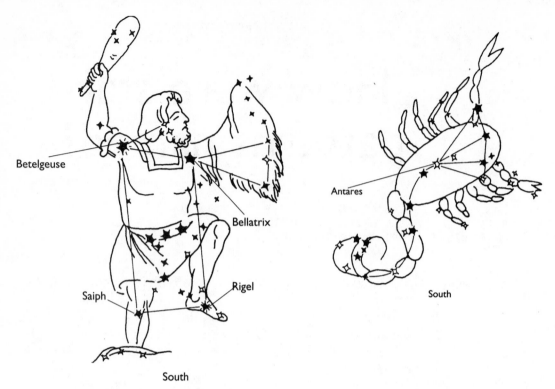

Betelgeuse

Bellatrix

Saiph

Rigel

South

16-1 Star configuration of Orion constellation.

Antares

South

16-2 Star configuration of Scorpius constellation.

reddish star. This is Antares (FIG. 16-2), and it is the basis for another constellation. Do you know the name of this constellation?

○ All signs of the Zodiac are star constellations.

Experiment 17

How are stars classified?

Materials   ❐ A pair of binoculars

Procedure   1. Locate the constellations that were described in Experiment 16.
2. Notice the different colors of the stars Antares or Betelgeuse.
3. Examine another star in the same constellation. For example, look at Bellatrix in Orion.

Results   Stars are classified according to their color, brightness, and age (FIG. 17-1). The color can range from red to white, depending on the temperature of the star's surface. Red stars, for example, are cooler than white hot stars.

Star	Type	Temperature (°K)	Color
Rigel	B8	12,000	Blue
Sirius	A0	10,000	Blue-white
Altair	A7	8,200	White
Our Sun	G2	5,800	Yellow
Arcturus	K0	4,500	Orange
Betelgeuse	M2	3,400	Red
Barnard's star	M6	3,000	Red

°K = degrees Kelvin
The Kelvin temperature scale can be determined by:

$$°K = °C + 273$$
$$°C = 5/9 \times (°F–32)$$
$$°F = \text{degrees Fahrenheit}$$

17-1   Star classification chart.

The brightness of a star produces some interesting star names. Weak or faint stars are known as *dwarfs,* while bright stars are called *giants.* Based on these two classifications, Antares and Betelgeuse are red giants. What does this tell you about Antares and Betelgeuse?

The final quality of a star deals with its age. Most stars, including our sun, go through an aging process. Currently, our sun is a yellow dwarf. As more of its fuel is used, it will turn into a red giant. Finally, the sun will end its life as a white dwarf.

Sometimes stars that are larger than our sun will have a different ending. After collapsing, these large suns explode in a *supernova.* There are times when this collapse doesn't result in an explosion. When this happens, a *black hole* is formed.

Further studies   Locate the stars in FIG. 17-1 and make two charts: one that classifies the stars according to their color and another that classifies the stars with reference to their brightness. Are the two charts the same? Which is the brightest star?

Did you know?   ◯ The Earth is about 93,000,000 miles from the Sun.

Experiment 18

How do comets travel?

Materials   ❏ Tennis ball
         ❏ Several feet of heavy string

Procedure
1. Tie one end of the string around the tennis ball.
2. Slowly swing the ball around your head.
3. As the ball picks up speed, let several inches of string pass through your hand. The ball should now be swinging farther away from your head.
4. Continue to let out string until the ball is 5 feet away from your head.

Results   A comet is an enormous, frozen, rocky body that orbits through the solar system. Several known comets have orbits in our solar system. The most famous of these is Halley's Comet (FIG. 18-1).

Comets are labeled according to the length of time it takes them to make a single orbit through the solar system. These orbits are known as *periods*. The period for Halley's Comet is 77 years. (Actually, the gravity of Jupiter affects the true period, so 74 to 79 years is the accepted Halley's Comet period). Other comets have shorter periods, such as the 3.3-year period of Encke's Comet. Still other comets have lengthy periods that make the verification of their existence difficult. Donati's Comet has one of the longer periods; it takes 2,040 years for it to travel around the solar system. These long orbits are equivalent to the longer string between your arm and the swinging tennis ball. The more string you feed through your fingers, the longer it will take the tennis ball to swing around your head.

18-1 Simulation of Halley's Comet as it appeared from Canada in 1986.

Further studies   Halley's Comet made its most recent appearance in 1986. By all accounts, the visual sightings of this famous comet were disappointing. Why was Halley's Comet missing its former luster? A good sighting of Halley's Comet was possible only in specific areas on Earth. Where were these areas? Why was the view of this comet restricted to these areas?

The vapor trail of Halley's Comet lacks the intensity that it demonstrated in 1910. Why was the comet's tail reduced?

Halley's Comet consists mainly of frozen gases. What would have happened if Halley's Comet had accidentally struck the Earth?

Did you know?   ○ In 1910, the Earth passed through Halley's Comet's tail. The effect of passing through the comet's tail was minimal, as the Earth's magnetic field acted as a shield.

Part 3
The Young Chemist

Two benefits can come from the changes that can happen to a particular substance or group of substances that are undergoing a chemical reaction: the production of new substances and the generation of usable energy. Linked with the changes that substances can undergo are the properties that can cause these changes. Changes between substances will not occur unless the properties between them are correct for the reaction. In other words, the properties control the change. Finally, knowing the structure of a substance is important in developing methods for controlling its future change. The structure of a substance in chemistry is expressed as a chemical formula. Combining the structure, properties, and changes of substances is the basis of chemistry.

Experiment 19

How can battery poles be identified?

Materials
- ❒ 6-volt battery
- ❒ Two 12-inch pieces of 18-gauge copper wire
- ❒ One potato

Procedure

1. Attach one of the wires to each of the poles of the battery (FIG. 19-1).
2. Cut the potato in half.
3. With its cut surface facing up, lay the potato on a table.
4. Place the battery next to the potato.
5. Insert the wires into the potato 1 inch apart (FIG. 19-2).

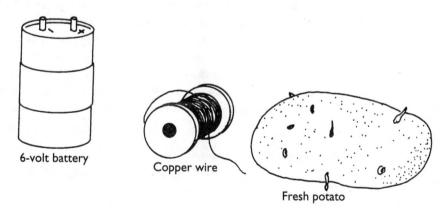

6-volt battery

Copper wire

Fresh potato

19-1 Materials needed for battery pole experiment.

Results   The wire connected to the positive pole of the battery will turn the potato green. The wire connected to the negative pole of the battery will form bubbles on the cut surface of the potato. Each of the reactions on the potato is caused by the movement of electrons from the

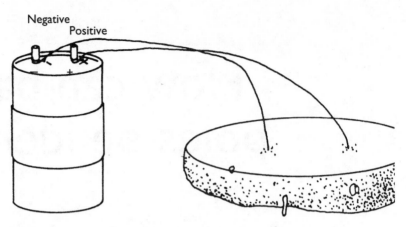

Negative
Positive

19-2 Results of battery pole experiment.

battery through the positive and negative poles. The potato's juice serves as the connection between two poles. A green color is formed on the pole from the ionization of the copper wire with the electrons from the potato juice. The bubbles from the negative pole wire are hydrogen gas. Hydrogen is released as the electrons flow into the negative pole.

Further studies   An ionic solution and paper can be substituted for the potato in this positive/negative pole test. Just place the wires on a piece of paper and add several drops of the solution between the two wire ends. After several minutes, you should be able to label the two poles of the battery. You can use table salt and water, vinegar, or lemon for the ionic solutions. Can you think of other ionic solutions? What would happen if these solutions were placed on the cut surface of the potato? Would you still be able to identify the positive and negative poles?

Did you know?   ○ Volta's first battery was a pile consisting of alternating layers of zinc and copper separated by moistened cardboard.

Experiment 20

How do crystals differ?

Materials
- ❏ Three small glass bowls
- ❏ Three dishwasher-safe measuring containers
- ❏ Three glass jars
- ❏ Salt
- ❏ Alum
- ❏ Epsom salt
- ❏ Water

Procedure

1. Examine the materials necessary for the experiment, then heat 1 cup of water.
2. Pour this water into a glass jar, and label the jar "Salt Solution."
3. Add salt to this water. Stir this solution while you are adding the salt.
4. Continue to add salt to the water until the salt doesn't dissolve in the solution. Salt will drop to the bottom of the bowl when you have reached this point. Additional stirring will not dissolve salt.

5. Place a lid on the jar, and let this solution cool to room temperature.
6. Repeat steps 1 through 5 for the alum and the Epsom salt, labeling each jar accordingly.
7. Pour small amounts from each of the cooled jars into its own separate glass bowl. Label each bowl accordingly.
8. Place all three of these bowls in a warm, quiet place. (Save the jars and their solutions, too.)
9. As the water from the solution evaporates, small crystals will form. NOTE: This might take several days.
10. Remove several of these crystals and dry them on some paper.
11. Clean the glass bowls.

12. Add fresh solution from each cooled jar into its correctly labeled bowl.
13. Place one of the small dried crystals on the bottom of the bowl. Make sure that the salt crystal is added to the salt solution, and so on.
14. After several days, remove the completed crystal from its solution.

Results   You should be able to observe some unique crystal shapes from this experiment. The salt, alum, and Epsom salt each have a distinctive crystal pattern (FIG. 20-1). The patterns were formed by growing the crystals in a *supersaturated solution,* or a liquid solution that is so full of a chemical compound that no more of the compound can be dissolved into the liquid. By adding salt (or alum or Epsom salt) to the water until the salt would not dissolve anymore, a supersaturated solution was formed. Slowly the water was removed through evaporation, leav-

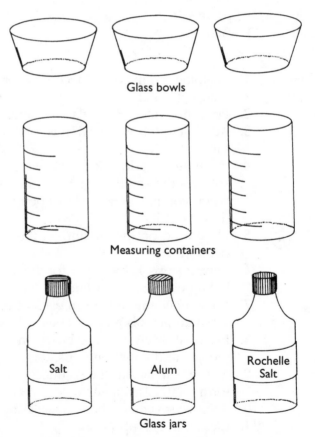

Glass bowls

Measuring containers

Salt   Alum   Rochelle Salt

Glass jars

20-1 Materials required for crystal-growing experiment.

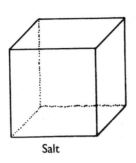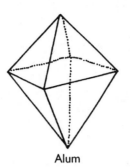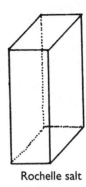

Salt   Alum   Rochelle salt

20-2 Three crystal structures.

ing only the crystals behind. These crystals attach to each other and form the large shapes that you saved in Step 14. This process of making crystals is called *crystallization*.

Further studies   Can other chemical compounds make crystals? Use the same procedure described above, and dissolve other chemicals in the water of Step 3. Compare the shape of these crystals to those that you made in this experiment. Are any of the crystals the same shape? Can you label each chemical based on its crystal structure?

Did you know?   ○ Modern radios rely on commercially grown crystals that contain traces of arsenic or gallium, for example.

How are sugar crystals shaped?

Materials
- ❑ Sugar
- ❑ Water
- ❑ Dishwasher-safe measuring container
- ❑ Large glass jar
- ❑ String
- ❑ Drinking straw
- ❑ Three metal washers
- ❑ Cardboard

Procedure
1. Heat 1 cup of water.
2. Add sugar until a supersaturated solution is produced. (This will take a lot of sugar: One cup of water can hold two cups of sugar.) A supersaturated sugar solution will be a thick syrup.
3. Clean the three metal washers.
4. Tie a piece of string to each of the washers.
5. Tie the other end of the string to the drinking straw.
6. Pour the sugar solution into the large jar.
7. Lower the washers into the sugar solution. Place the straw across the top of the jar to suspend the string and washers in the sugar solution.
8. Cover the jar with the cardboard, as shown in FIG. 21-1, and leave it alone for one week.

Results
After one week, sugar crystals will form on the string as the water evaporates. The crystals enlarge as more sugar attaches to the string. When the crystals are fully developed, remove them from the jar and dry them (FIG. 21-2). Compare the crystals you created in this experiment with the ones you created in Experiment 20. What conclusions can you make about crystal structure based on these two experiments?

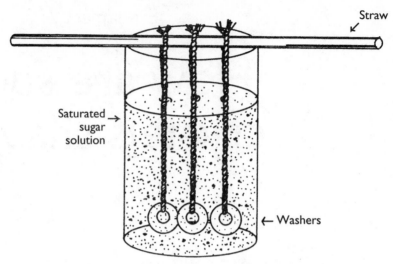

21-1 Procedure for growing crystals.

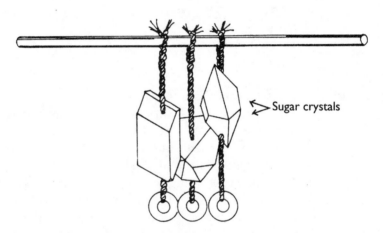

21-2 Results from growing crystals.

Further studies Use a hand lens to examine some granular sugar. How does the shape of the sugar grains compare with the crystals that you made? Perform the same hand-lens comparison on the salt, alum, and Epsom salt, and compare them to the crystals made in Experiment 20. What do you notice about the shape of these compounds versus the shape of their crystals?

Did you know? ○ Rock candy is really large sugar crystals that have been grown on string.

Experiment 22

How does film make negatives?

Materials ❐ One pack of Type 667 Polaroid film
❐ Dark room
❐ Penny
❐ Pencil
❐ Small piece of window screen

Procedure

1. Turn out the lights in the room. The room must be completely dark.
2. Carefully open the Polaroid film pack.
3. Pull a single sheet of Polaroid film out of the open film pack.
4. Lay this piece of film on a flat surface so the emulsion or picture-taking side is facing up.

5. Place the penny, pencil, and window screen on the film's emulsion.
6. Quickly turn the room's lights on and then off again.
7. Following the exposure, develop the Polaroid film. This is a difficult procedure that can only be learned through experience. First, fold the film's carrier sheet over the top of the film's emulsion. The film should now be covered. Next, locate the pod of developing solution. This is a bulge that is near the paper hinge for the emulsion and carrier sheet. After you have found this pod, take the pencil and squeeze this bag until it breaks. The developer is now leaking out of its pod. Push the developer across the face of the emulsion by rolling the pencil behind the developer.
8. Leave the developer in contact with the emulsion for 30 seconds.
9. Turn on the room's lights.
10. Peel the carrier sheet away from the photographic print.
11. Throw the carrier sheet away and let the print air dry (FIG. 22-1).

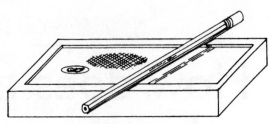

22-1 Procedures for making a photogram.

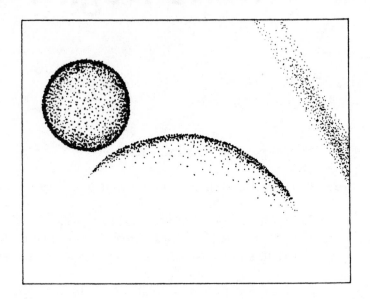

22-2 Simulated photogram.

Results The photographic print will show the dark outline of the penny, pencil, and window screen (FIG. 22-2). This type of print is called a *photogram*. There is no need for a camera or a lens when making
photograms. Objects (such as the penny, pencil, and window screen
in this experiment) are placed in direct contact with an emulsion.
Light-sensitive silver nitrate crystals are held in the emulsion. The
subsequent contact with light exposes the film's silver nitrate crystals.
These exposed crystals undergo a chemical reaction to the light, depending on the amount of light that strikes each crystal. Later, the
film's developer has a reaction with the exposed silver nitrate and
turns the crystals into metallic silver. For this reason, black or shad-
owed objects stay dark on the final print, while lighter areas turn
white (FIGS. 22-3 and 22-4).

22-3 Example of photogram made from fabric.

22-4 Using exposure, developer, and selective development leads to creative photograms.

Further studies If you find the Polaroid film and its development to be too difficult, Kodak makes a film that is simpler to use. Kodak Studio Proof is a photosensitive paper that acts just like a Polaroid film, with two major differences. First, this emulsion can be exposed only by direct sunlight, so you can safely handle this paper in an ordinary room and the indoor lights won't ruin your pictures. Second, you can develop Kodak Studio Proof in running tap water. The running-water bath actually washes all of the remaining silver nitrate crystals off the paper. However, the resulting image will gradually fade unless you soak the washed paper print in a tray of photographic fixer (fixer is also known as *hypo*). The best fixer for Kodak Studio Proof is a solution of sodium thiosulfate. Use the following times for experimenting with Kodak Studio Proof:

Exposure: 2–5 minutes in direct sunlight.
Development: 10–15 minutes in 70-degree running water.
Fixing: 3–5 minutes in sodium thiosulfate; mix ½ pound of sodium thiosulfate in 1 quart of water.

Wear safety goggles while fixing the paper. CAUTION: Do not let the sodium thiosulfate remain in contact with your skin! Be sure to wash your hands frequently.

Did you know? ○ Reverend Hannibal Williston invented celluloid photographic film and received the patent for it in 1887.

Experiment 23

How do emulsions work?

Materials
- [ ] 1 ounce ferric ammonium citrate
- [ ] ½ ounce potassium ferricyanide
- [ ] 1 cup water
- [ ] Three glass containers
- [ ] Small piece of canvas
- [ ] Penny, pencil, and/or other object with which to make print (see Experiment 22)

CAUTION: These materials are dangerous; follow all directions accurately. Do not get any chemicals in your eyes! If you accidentally do, flush your eyes immediately with water. As a precaution, wear your safety goggles.

Procedure

1. Mix 1 ounce of ferric ammonium citrate with ½ cup of water.
2. In a separate container, mix ½ ounce of potassium ferricyanide with ½ cup of water. (These chemical solutions don't become light-sensitive until they are mixed together.)
3. In the third container, stir together 1 ounce of each solution.
4. Paint some paper with this solution. Special-coated papers, such as canvas, work best.
5. Let the painted paper dry.
6. Expose the paper and objects like you did with the Kodak Studio Proof paper. Leave your emulsion in the direct sunlight until the image turns dark blue.
7. Wash the print in running water for 10 to 15 minutes.
8. Allow your print to dry (FIG. 23-1).

Further studies
Some chemical compounds are light-sensitive. When they are exposed to light, the energy absorbed causes a chemical reaction (in this case,

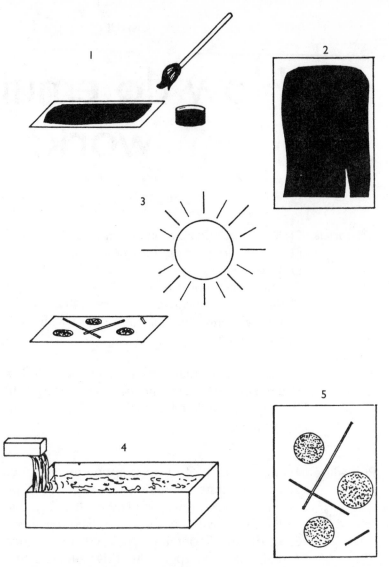

23-1 Procedures for making your own emulsion.

it causes the emulsion to become water-soluble). Research other light-sensitive emulsions such as those used on TRI-X or T-max black-and-white films. What makes them different?

Did you know? ○ Edwin Land invented the Polaroid Land camera, the first commercially available camera to develop the film inside the camera itself.

Experiment 24

How does emulsion-coated paper work?

Another exciting photographic emulsion that is simple to mix and develop involves the gum-bichromate process. The steps in this process are similar to those in the previous photographic emulsion explanation (see Experiment 23).

Materials
- [ ] 1 ounce gum arabic
- [ ] ½ ounce bichromate
- [ ] 1 ounce lampblack powder
- [ ] 7 ounces water
- [ ] Three glass containers
- [ ] One sheet sized paper
- [ ] Paintbrush

Procedure

1. Mix the 1 ounce of gum arabic with 2 ounces of water.
2. In the second container, mix the ½ ounce of bichromate with 5 ounces of water.
3. Combine 3 ounces of each mixture together in the third container. This is your emulsion.
4. Add the lampblack to this emulsion, and mix all of the ingredients thoroughly.
5. Paint the emulsion on a sheet of sized paper. (*Sized paper* refers to paper that has had its pores filled with a fluid coating. You can add common household spray starch to regular paper for a good sizing substitute.)
6. Let the painted paper air-dry in a dark room.
7. Expose and develop your gum-bichromate print in the same manner as stated in the previous photographic emulsion experiment (see Experiment 23).

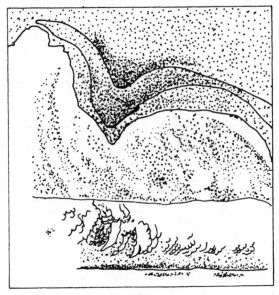

24-1 Various layers of emulsions can be added to paper for an interesting photogram.

8. Air-dry the developed gum-bichromate print (FIG. 24-1).

Further studies How does this print compare to the print you made in Experiment 23? Instead of using solid objects, try making some prints of transparent, translucent, or porous objects (plastic objects, wire mesh, etc.).

Did you know? ○ The English scientist Sir William Crookes' complaint about photographic plates being fogged in his laboratory led to the discovery of X rays.

Part 4
The Young Meteorologist

The exact role that other sciences play in meteorology depends on the type of weather study that is being performed. For example, predicting the smog levels in a large city would require the use of chemistry, life sciences, mathematics, and physics. In this example, chemistry would be needed to evaluate the composition of the air pollution; the life sciences would be used to determine the effect that the predicted smog level would have on the average human being; mathematics would provide an accurate statement of the length of time that the smog would remain a danger to the city's residents; and, finally, physics would help in understanding the cause for the increased smog level. Clearly, meteorology is a complex science that depends on the knowledge gained through other scientific disciplines.

Experiment 25

How does fog form?

Materials
- ❑ Medium-sized glass jar
- ❑ Hot water
- ❑ Ice cube (big enough to cover jar's mouth)

Procedure
1. Fill one-half of the glass jar with hot water.
2. Lay the ice cube over the mouth of the jar. The ice cube should cover most of the jar's opening.
3. Observe the formation of fog inside the jar.

Results Fog is a low-altitude cloud. In order for fog to form, the air must be saturated with water vapor and the air's temperature must fall below its dew point. When both of these conditions are met, fog will form in one of two types. The first type is called an *advection fog*, which is formed when a warm, saturated air mass passes over a cool ground or cool body of water. The other type is called a *radiation fog*, which occurs when the ground quickly loses or radiates its heat into the air. This radiation of heat causes the ground to cool rapidly and condense the moisture in the warmer upper air.

Further studies Which type of fog did you create in this experiment? Can you create an experiment that will form an advection fog? You will need a warm, moist air source and a cool surface. One way of thinking about this problem is to study a pot that is boiling water. As the water boils, it produces steam. Is there any similarity between the steam from boiling water and an advection fog?

Experiment 26

How does the wind blow?

Materials
- ❐ Candle
- ❐ Soap bubbles
- ❐ Match

Procedure
1. Light the candle with the match.
2. Gently blow some soap bubbles. Let these bubbles float in the direction of the candle's flame.

3. Watch the bubbles as they draw closer to the flame.
4. Blow additional soap bubbles around the flame and watch their behavior.

Results Wind is an air current. Air currents are generated by contact between warm and cold air masses. In your experiment, the soap bubbles rode the warm air currents (the air close to the flame) until the cooler air (the air farthest from the flame) made them fall. This observation points out that air temperature also changes the air's pressure. It is the combination of these two effects that make warm and cold air masses produce wind. In the atmosphere, these differences in temperature and pressure cause enormous currents to be formed between the warm equatorial air and the cold arctic air.

Further studies In 1805, Sir Francis Beaufort designed a table of wind speeds called the Beaufort Wind Scale (FIG. 26-1). This table was used by sailors to determine the maximum power for sailing. Use this scale for judging the speed of the wind in your location.

Beaufort Scale Number	Wind	Speed (mph)
0	Calm	0–1
1	Light	1–3
2	Slight	4–7
3	Gentle	8–12
4	Moderate	13–18
5	Fresh	19–24
6	Strong	25–31
7	Moderate gale	32–38
8	Fresh gale	39–46
9	Strong gale	47–54
10	Whole gale	55–63
11	Storm	64–75
12	Hurricane	75+

26-1 The Beaufort scale of wind speeds.

Did you know? ○ The world's windiest place is The Commonwealth Bay, George V Coast, Antarctica, where winds reach 200 miles per hour!

Experiment 27

How is rain made?

Materials
- ❐ Large glass plate
- ❐ Freezer
- ❐ Cooking pot
- ❐ Water

Procedure

1. Place the large glass plate inside a freezer.
2. Heat the water in the cooking pot until it is boiling.
3. While wearing safety goggles and gloves, remove the glass plate and hold it over the boiling water.
4. Slightly tilt the plate as the condensation forms on its surface.

Results

Rain is the product of moisture-saturated clouds. As water vapor-saturated air begins to cool clouds develop. If this cooling continues and moisture is still present inside the air, water droplets will form. Then the water droplets will slowly begin to attach to one another, and large raindrops will begin to fill the air inside the cloud. When these drops of water are too big to be held aloft by air currents, they will fall to the ground, an effect known as *rain*.

Further studies

Rainfall is usually measured with a *rain gauge*. This special tube measures the amount of rainfall as a percentage of an inch. Can you construct a rain gauge? Do your units of measurement compare with those found on a true rain gauge? What if it rains several inches? Can your rain gauge accurately measure such large volumes? How could a simple rain gauge be designed that would reliably measure rainfall up to 10 inches?

Did you know? ○ Mount Waialeale, Kauai, Hawaii, has about 350 rainy days each year.

How is snowfall measured?

Materials
- ❒ Snow
- ❒ Large bucket
- ❒ Rain gauge
- ❒ Spoon

Procedure
1. Fill a large bucket with snow from a heavy, wet snowfall.
2. Place 3 inches of snow inside the rain gauge. Be sure that you don't pack the snow into the gauge. Try to fill the rain gauge in a manner similar to the way the snow fell on the ground.
3. Melt the snow inside the rain gauge.
4. Measure the indicated amount of water. Record this number. Repeat the same procedure for a dry, light snowfall. Record your final melted-snow moisture amount.

Results
On the average, snow holds much less water than rain, so it takes more snow to produce an amount of water equal to that produced by rain. The type of snow also affects the amount of moisture produced. For example, 6 inches of a moist snow is equal to 1 inch of rain. Alternatively, 30 inches of dry, light snow is equal to 1 inch of rain.

The formation of snow closely follows that of rain. The major difference between these two forms of precipitation is that snow results when water droplets freeze inside the moisture-saturated cloud before they fall to the ground.

Each flake of snow is a six-sided crystal that can have any shape (FIG. 28-1). The freezing and air current inside the cloud make each flake shape different. This means that no two snow crystals have exactly the same shape.

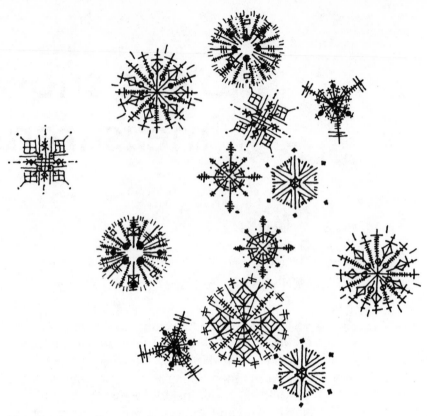

28-1 For fun, see if you can find the odd snowflake.

Further studies   In 1946, Vincent J. Schaefer produced the first artificial snow. See if you can repeat Schaefer's experiment. Schaefer blew his warm, moist breath into a deep-freezer. He then quickly placed an extremely cold rod directly inside the steam clouds that his breath had made. The result was snow.

Did you know?   ○ The coldest measured average temperature is −70 degrees Fahrenheit at Plateau Station, Antarctica.

Part 5
The Young Biologist

Biology is the science of animals and plants and their life processes. One of the first biologists was the Greek Anaximander in 600 B.C. His theory was that all biological creatures evolved from water. Another Greek, Theophrastus, performed the first work in *botany,* which is the science of plants and their life processes.

The science of heredity and plant and animal variation is called *genetics.* Much of the genetic technique performed today was first practiced by Gregor Johann Mendel in the 1860s. Mendel's work in genetics gave rise to the theory of gene transfer of plant and animal variation.

A biology branch that studies only microscopic plants and animals is called *microbiology.* Much of microbiological work centers around the control of bacteria and viruses through antibiotics and enzymes.

Physiology examines the functions and processes of plants and animals at the cell level. Two offshoots of physiology are occasionally referred to as sciences: *anatomy* and *biochemistry.* All three of these studies contribute to the study of disease and the advancement of medicine.

Finally, *zoology* deals exclusively with animals and their classification. Many of the more famous scientists were zoologists. Aristotle, Linnaeus, Huxley, Darwin, and Pavlov all contributed to the classification of the animal kingdom.

From each of these short descriptions of biological fields, you can derive a common theme: Each one involves the study of life.

Experiment 29

How does pond water appear to "move?"

Materials   ❏ 1 gallon standing water (regular tap water that has been standing for several days)
❏ 2-gallon glass jar with lid
❏ Small glass jar with lid
❏ Hand lens
❏ Small scoop

Procedure   1. Travel to a local freshwater pond.
2. Scoop up some of the bottom debris from the pond. This debris can be rotting leaves, scum, or plant material.
3. Place the sample in the small glass jar.
4. Add a small portion of pond water to your sample. This should be just enough water to keep the bottom debris moist.
5. When you return to your laboratory, fill the large glass jar with the standing water.
6. Carefully lift the bottom debris from the small jar and place it in the large, water-filled jar.
7. Place this jar in a brightly lit area, but avoid direct sunlight.

Results   After about 24 hours, the water should be moving and teeming with life. Use your hand lens to inspect the water. The movement in the water is from small, one-celled animals called *protozoans*. Protozoans are *invertebrates*, or animals that lack an internal spinal cord. Even though a protozoan is a single-celled animal, it still is capable of performing functions similar to our own: feeding, breathing, and reproduction.

Over 30,000 Protozoa species can be found in freshwater. Protozoa actually comprise a phylum in the animal kingdom of which there are

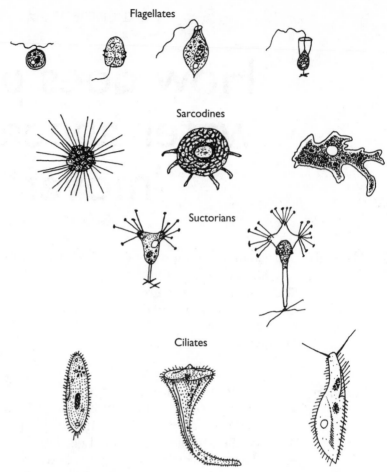

29-1 Four types of protozoa.

four more groups divided according to the way they move: *flagellates,* which have long hair-like projections called *flagella; sarcodines,* which are single-celled animals with *pseudopodia; suctoria,* which are protozoans with tentacles; and *ciliates,* which are the most complex one-celled animals (FIG. 29-1).

Further studies You can easily turn your protozoan aquarium into an invertebrate zoo simply by feeding these single-celled creatures. An excellent food source is malted milk powder. Add only a small portion (less than ⅛ teaspoon) to the top of your aquarium, and the powder will form bacteria that the protozoans eat. Avoid using too much powder or you will pollute the water. Your protozoans will need to be fed only once every 1 to 2 weeks.

One of the greatest drawbacks with your invertebrate zoo is that the animals are so hard to see. Can you think of a technique for making them more visible? One way to do this is to "paint" your protozoans by adding a dye to their food supply. Adding ordinary food dye to the malted milk powder will make some of the tiny invertebrates show their true colors.

Be warned that this method can color the water. If that happens, collect as many of the protozoa as possible and place them in a small holding jar. After cleaning and refilling your main glass jar, pour the protozoan-laden water back into your zoo.

Another compound you can add to the water to color your invertebrates is powdered carmine. Any protozoan that eats the carmine will turn pink or red.

Experiment 30

How do animals' feet differ?

Materials
- ❐ Plaster of paris
- ❐ Cardboard
- ❐ Masking tape
- ❐ Mixing bowl
- ❐ Spoon
- ❐ Water

Procedure
1. Locate an animal's footprint in dirt or mud. (You can produce one artificially by gently pressing a dog's or cat's paw into some soft mud.) Allow the mud to harden before you continue with this experiment.
2. Blow any loose dirt and plant material away from the track.
3. Curve the cardboard into a tube so that it fits around the animal's track. Hold the cardboard together with a piece of masking tape.
4. Firmly press the cardboard ring into the dirt surrounding the animal track.
5. Fix the plaster of paris with the water in the mixing bowl.
6. Pour the plaster mixture over the animal track.
7. Use the spoon to smooth the surface of the plaster.
8. Let the plaster harden.
9. Remove the cardboard ring and lift the plaster cast off the animal track.

Results
The plaster of paris should have made a perfect cast of the animal track—a three-dimensional model of the animal's foot. Compare this model with the animal's actual foot.

Feet are used primarily as a method of transportation. Actually, the leg is the main source of movement and power, the foot makes contact with the ground. Therefore, an animal's foot must reflect the size of the animal (an elephant's foot is larger than a lizard's), the mode of travel (a lion needs a foot for running, and a frog needs a foot for jumping), and the type of terrain (a mountain goat needs a hoof, and a seal needs a flipper).

Further studies Make a plaster cast of several different feet. Make several comparisons of your plaster track collection. Which foot is the largest? Which foot is the smallest? Can you identify the animal based on the shape of its foot? Try making tracks with your plaster cast. Compare these tracks with the animal's real track. Are they exactly the same? Can you tell the two track types apart?

Experiment 31

How do animals survive?

Materials
- ☐ Nine blindfolds
- ☐ Two whistles
- ☐ Two bells
- ☐ Two wooden sticks
- ☐ Two rattles

Procedure
1. This experiment requires 10 people.
2. Assign the following titles to each person:

1 person	judge or referee
1 person	the predator
8 people	the prey

3. Each prey is given one of the noisemakers. Each noisemaker pair (for example, the two whistles), represents prey of the same species. Therefore, there are four different species in this experiment.
4. All of the participants, except for the judge, are blindfolded.
5. When the referee starts the experiment, the rules are as follows:
   a. The predator stalks the prey. When the predator touches a prey, it removes the blindfold from the trapped prey. This person now sits out and watches the rest of the experiment.
   b. The prey must avoid the predator. Contact with the predator will end the experiment for any member.
   c. The prey must also locate other members of its species. When one prey touches its species' counterpart, the referee removes the blindfolds from both prey members. These two members are also "out," and can now watch the rest of the experiment.
6. The experiment continues until no prey remains. This loss of prey can result from the prey being eaten by the predator or, the prey finding its species' counterparts.

Results This experiment represents the life-and-death struggle faced by all animals on a daily basis (FIG. 31-1). The pedator must locate food or prey in order to survive. The prey, on the other hand, must locate other members of the same species so they can reproduce.

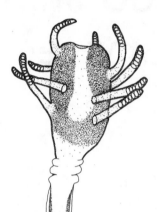

31-1 A freshwater predator, Cordylophora lacustris.

You can learn a number of things about survival from this experiment. First, a successful predator must be silent. A predator stalking her or his prey must rely on surprise to ensure a "kill." Second, prey that are too intent on locating a mate will be easily caught by a predator. Prey in a real food chain must balance all of their activities against the risk of being eaten. Finally, prey can't be too noisy when looking for their mate. In nature, animals never make continuous noise because this would make them easy targets for a predator. Instead, an animal will selectively use its noise-making ability to locate other members of its own kind.

For these reasons, the best way to approach this experiment is for the prey to make a short noise, and then wait for a reply. When the reply is heard, the prey should travel a short distance in that direction and then make another noise. Repeating these steps will bring the other species members together without attracting the attention of the predator.

Further studies You can be modify this experiment for nighttime. Blindfolds are not necessary when conducting this experiment at night, but several of the prey members should be equipped with different-colored flashlights. How can the prey species that are using flashlights find each other without attracting the attention of the predator?

Some predators hunt in packs. Perform this experiment with several predators after a limited number of prey. What are the results? Do some of the predators starve? How do these experiments apply to nature?

Did you know?   ○ Predators are either *nocturnal* (night) hunters or *diurnal* (day) hunters.

Experiment 32

How do earthworms learn?

Materials
- ❏ 10-x-17-x-⅛-inch sheet of plywood
- ❏ Saw
- ❏ White glue
- ❏ Small nails
- ❏ Hand-powered drill and drill bit
- ❏ Sandpaper
- ❏ 30-inch length of 18-gauge solid wire
- ❏ Battery holder
- ❏ Four AA batteries
- ❏ Cardboard

Procedure

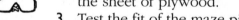

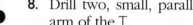

1. Draw the maze dimensions from FIG. 32-1 on the sheet of plywood.
2. While wearing safety goggles, cut the nine maze pieces from the sheet of plywood.
3. Test the fit of the maze pieces. Sand any edges that fit poorly.
4. Apply white glue to an edge of the main maze T piece.
5. Place the plywood side against the white glue.
6. Secure this side with several small nails.
7. Repeat steps 4 through 6 for each maze side piece.
8. Drill two, small, parallel holes along the bottom edge in one arm of the T.
9. Cut two 12-inch lengths of wire. Strip 3 inches of insulation off one end of each wire.
10. Run a bare wire end through each of the drilled holes in the plywood.
11. Connect the other end of each wire to the battery holder.
12. Cut a small rectangle of cardboard and place it under the parallel bare wire leads. This will act as insulation for the wire.
13. Insert the four AA batteries into the battery holder.

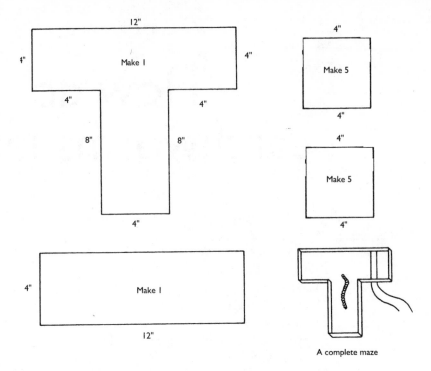

32-1 Procedures for building an earthworm maze.

14. Position the earthworm for testing at the bottom of the T.
15. Observe the results.

Results After several repetitions, the earthworm should avoid the exposed electric wires. When the earthworm moves over both of these wires at the sandpaper end, a small electrical shock is produced. This shock will *condition* or train the earthworm to avoid the T arm with the electrical wires.

An earthworm is able to learn limited sense repetitions due to two enlarged nerves in its head. These nerve clumps are called *ganglia*. In addition to these elementary brains, the earthworm also has an extensive nervous system, which enables the earthworm to react to artificial pressure stimuli.

Further studies Test the other sensory abilities of the earthworm. Is the earthworm sensitive to light? Does the earthworm react to sound? Based on these data, what can you say about the overall intelligence of an earthworm?

Did you know? ○ The common earthworm has about 100 segments.

Experiment 33

How do crayfish breathe?

Materials   ❏   One living crayfish
         ❏   Tray to hold crayfish
         ❏   Water
         ❏   Medicine dropper
         ❏   Red food coloring

Procedure   1. If you are unable to locate a suitable live crayfish yourself, you may order a suitable specimen from a biological supply house.
         2. Fill the tray with water.
         3. Place the crayfish in the tray of water.
         4. Hold the crayfish upside down on the bottom of the tray. This procedure might be extremely difficult to perform. If you are unable to persuade your specimen to sit in this position, try the remainder of the experiment with the crayfish in an upright posture.
         5. Fill the medicine dropper with red food coloring.
         6. Gently squeeze two drops of food coloring behind the last leg pair of the crayfish. Repeat this process for both leg pairs.
         7. Observe the food coloring.

Results   The cloud of red food coloring is quickly pulled inside the crayfish's *exoskeleton*. The entry point is at the base of the large body cover or *carapace*. You should be able to see little jets of food coloring slowly exiting near the head of the crayfish. The actual exit for the dye is at two points near the base of each antenna (FIG. 33-1). This entire process is a demonstration of the crayfish's respiratory system.

       The *respiratory system* is the group of organs responsible for breathing. A creature that breathes underwater, like the crayfish, needs a special respiratory organ—in this case, the gills. In operation, water enters the crayfish's gill region from under the rear of its carapace. After

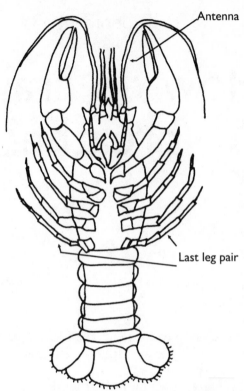

Antenna

Last leg pair

33-1 Dye entry points on the underside of a crayfish.

moving through its gills, the water leaves the crayfish over its gills. The crayfish needs a constant flow of water over its gills. This movement brings fresh water full of oxygen in contact with the gills. The gills then remove the oxygen from the water. Finally, the used water leaves the gills. This process is repeated for every breath that the crayfish takes.

Further studies Many different freshwater aquatic animals use gills. Can you name 10 species that have gills? How do each of these animals direct the water over their gills? Use the food-coloring test to determine the exact flow of water through the animal's respiratory system.

Another exciting feature of the crayfish is its ability to leave the water. This departure from water is limited to several minutes. How is the gill-breathing animal able to leave the water? Can a fish leave the water for several minutes? What is the crayfish's secret?

Did you know? ○ Crayfish have the ability to grow new body parts if they lose one (claw or leg, for example).

How do tadpoles change into frogs?

Materials
- ❑ Several young tadpoles
- ❑ 10-gallon aquarium
- ❑ Water
- ❑ Aerator
- ❑ Water plants
- ❑ Hand lens
- ❑ Pencil and notebook

Procedures
1. Collect several young tadpoles that do not yet have visible legs. If you cannot find such young samples, you can raise tadpoles from live frog eggs or you can purchase tadpoles directly from a biological supply house.
2. Place your tadpoles in a 10-gallon aquarium with water, an aerator, and water plants.
3. Observe the tadpoles with your hand lens periodically for several weeks.
4. Make careful notes on your observations. Make a daily log entry on the appearance of each tadpole.
5. Continue observing the tadpoles until they change into adult frogs.

Results
A tadpole changes into an adult frog through a process known as *metamorphosis*. This change involves the transformation of an egg into a tadpole and, finally, into an adult frog. Actually, a frog's metamorphosis is termed an *incomplete metamorphosis*, while a butterfly's *complete metamorphosis* transformation. The difference between these two metamorphic processes is the presence of the butterfly's pupae stage, sometimes erroneously called the butterfly's "cocoon" (FIG. 34-1). The frog's incomplete metamorphosis lacks a similar pupae stage;

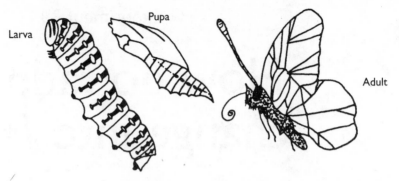

34-1 Larva, pupa, and adult stages of a butterfly (complete metamorphosis).

the tadpole is a combination of both the butterfly's pupa and larva stages (FIG. 34-2).

Metamorphosis is a lengthy process that begins in the egg stage where the young tadpole is formed. Following emergence from the egg, the young tadpole is unable to move very effectively. At this stage, the tadpole attaches itself to a solid object and feeds on algae. As the tadpole feeds, its head and tail begin to increase in size. Slowly, a pair of hind legs appear from the body near the base of the tail. As the hind legs develop, the gills are replaced by air-breathing lungs. This transformation means that the tadpole must come to the surface of the water to breathe. When the front legs begin to appear, the tadpole begins to lose its tail. Finally, an adult frog emerges from the water (FIG. 34-3).

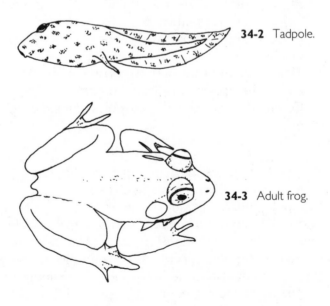

34-2 Tadpole.

34-3 Adult frog.

The entire metamorphic process can take from 2 months to 2 years, depending on the species of frog.

Further studies Raise other frog species. Compare the data of each species. Which frog requires the longest to change into an adult? Which frog has the biggest tadpole?

Metamorphosis is not limited to frogs. Other amphibians also undergo this change. Collect some toad and salamander eggs. Raise these eggs to adulthood and compare these data with your frog data. Which amphibian takes the longest to mature?

Did you know? ◯ The West African Goliath frog can jump almost 10 feet.

Experiment 35

How do ants live in colonies?

Materials
❏ Two 8-x-10-x-¼-inch sheets of glass
❏ One 3-sided 8-x-10-x-1-inch wood frame
❏ Window screen
❏ Utility scissors
❏ Plastic cement
❏ Soil
❏ 15 to 30 ants
❏ Cotton
❏ 4 tablespoons water
❏ 1 tablespoon sugar

Procedure
1. Prepare your ant farm by gluing the two sheets of glass on either side of the wood frame. (Be sure to follow the package instructions on the tube of glue to allow enough setting-up time.)
2. Fill the wood frame with soil (FIG. 35-1).

3. Using the utility scissors, cut a piece of a window screen to fit over the top of your ant farm as a lid.
4. Collect 15 to 30 ants from your neighborhood.
5. Place the ants inside the frame.
6. Combine the sugar and water. Then soak a piece of cotton in the sugar water, and drop the cotton on top of the soil.
7. Close the lid and observe your ant colony for a week.

Results
After several days, the ants will dig a small network through the soil. Most of your ants will be one of the three types of *workers*—the ants that lack wings and that can't lay eggs. The *standard worker* is found on the outside of the colony and is responsible for bringing food back to the colony. The *nurse worker* is a small ant that cares for the colony's eggs and can be found only inside an ant colony. The last type of worker is the *soldier*, easily identified by its large pincers. As

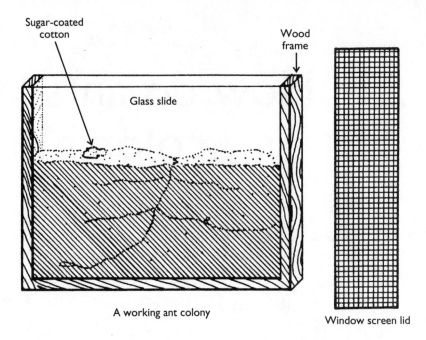

Sugar-coated cotton

Wood frame

Glass slide

A working ant colony

Window screen lid

35-1 Procedures for building an ant farm.

their name would suggest, soldiers defend the colony from its enemies. In an ant colony, tasks are evenly divided among these workers. This division in labor and tasks is only possible in the colony environment.

Further studies Ants react to other ants, as well as to tastes. Develop a series of experiments for your ant farm that will test the reactions of your ants. What happened when you introduced a strange ant into your ant farm? Do your ants prefer certain foods?

Observing your ant farm is also a good way to gather notes on the biology of ants. How do ants eat their food? How do your ants identify each other as colony members?

Did you know? ⭕ Insects vastly outnumber any other class of animals.

How are animal populations counted?

Materials
- ▣ 1-pound bag of rice
- ▣ Large open floor
- ▣ Tape measure
- ▣ Masking tape
- ☑ 12-x-12-inch-square wire frame
- ▣ Pencil and notebook

Procedure

1. Using a tape measure and the masking tape, mark your large floor into a 15-x-15-foot square (Don't write on the floor!).
2. Count the number of grains of rice in the 1-pound bag. (The best way to do this is to estimate the number in the whole bag by counting the number of grains in one ounce and multiplying by 16.)
3. Scatter the rice evenly throughout the 15-x-15-foot square.
4. Randomly drop the 12-x-12-inch wire frame on the ground that is covered with rice.
5. Count the number of rice grains within this grid.
6. Take several of these random counts.
7. Average your counts into a grain-per-grid value by adding each count total and then dividing that sum by the number of counts you made.
8. There are 225 grids within your 15-x-15-foot study area. Multiply this number by the average number of grains per grid, and you should come up with something close to the number of grains of rice in the 1-pound bag.

Results All of this number play relates to the statistics of animal populations. Several factors will affect your final rice count.

1. The number of random samples you make will determine the accuracy of your final value. The higher the number of random samples, the more accurate the final rice grain estimate will be.
2. Incomplete grain counting and arithmetic errors can also affect your results, but you can lessen these risks by taking careful notes at each step in this experiment.
3. The uniformity of the rice distribution will affect the final grain-count accuracy. If the grains of rice aren't equally spaced throughout the 15-x-15-foot area, the final estimate will be incorrect.

Perform this entire experiment several times and average all of your results. How does this average compare with the real number of rice grains? Why is this value closer than each of the individual population surveys?

Further studies You can apply the same population estimation techniques that you learned in the experiment to live plant and animal populations outdoors. In some cases, you might need to alter the dimensions of your test area, as well as the dimensions of your sampling grid (FIG. 36-1).

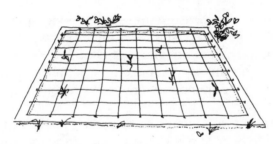

36-1 A grid for counting population density.

Sample the populations of grass in your lawn. What are the populations of the various grasses and weeds in your lawn? Study these populations over a period of time. What happens to the individual populations? Did one species dominate your lawn? Based on these data, can you predict what will happen to your lawn population next year?

Perform this same experiment with the tree population at your local park. Be sure to choose a park where it is impossible to actually count each tree.

Did you know? ○ Almost two-thirds of the world's population lies in 10 countries.

Part 6
The Young Physicist

The study of physics began with the Greek Democritus in approximately 400 B.C. Democritus stated that all matter was composed of tiny atoms—a statement that became the initial definition of the physical sciences. Even after 2,300 years, Democritus's definition remains true.

From this beginning, physics has grown into a major force in our daily lives. In addition, the physical sciences undergo constant change. As new disciplines of physics are discovered, they are placed under the physical sciences umbrella. Many of these additions have occurred through the discoveries of well-known, important scientists; people like Newton, Bernoulli, Faraday, Roentgen, Edison, and Einstein have all contributed to answering the "how" questions of life.

How are mirrors used in copiers?

Materials
- ❐ This book
- ❐ Photocopying machine

Procedure
1. The illustrations from this book for copying during this experiment.
2. Copy each illustration separately. (You do not have to copy all the illustrations.)
3. Compare your results.

Results Photocopiers use mirrors or a prism lens to reproduce the material that is being copied. This mirror reverses the image so that it will be an exact replica of the origin. Once you think about the photocopying process, the need for the mirror becomes obvious.

All photocopiers use light for exposing the original material. This exposure is made on a light-sensitive material, usually an electrically charged rotating drum or stationary plate. If the image from the original did not travel through a mirror, the resulting copy would be a *reverse-image negative*—in other words, a white-on-black image. Obviously, such a process would be unsatisfactory for producing exact copies. Therefore, the mirror is used to reverse the image prior to exposing the charged plate. Once the reversal is complete, the plate is charged with the image, the plate is coated with a powdered toner that accepts the charge, and a piece of paper is placed in contact with the plate. The charged particles of toner stick to the paper, and the copy is complete.

Further studies Try reading a book held up to a mirror. Now use a second mirror placed in a position between you and the first mirror. Can you read the book now? Periscopes on submarines and tanks need to use two mirrors. What would you see in a periscope if the second mirror were not there?

Did you know?   ○ The largest reflecting telescope in the United States is the 200-inch Hale reflector at Mount Palomar, California, completed in 1948.

Experiment 38

How are fiber optics used?

Materials
- ❐ Fiber-optic cable (Radio Shack Part No. 276-228)
- ❐ Small flashlight (Radio Shack Part No. 61-2626 or No. 61-2625)
- ❐ Colored filters
- ❐ Colored cellophane

Procedure
1. Hold one end of the fiber-optic cable over the front of the flashlight lens.
2. Turn on the flashlight.
3. Examine the other end of the fiber-optic cable.
4. Bend and twist the fiber-optic cable.
5. Place a colored filter between the end of the fiber-optic cable and the flashlight bulb.
6. Examine the other end of the fiber-optic cable.

Results Fiber-optic cable is able to transmit light in a tight, wire-like bundle. The average fiber-optic cable is made of several glass or plastic filaments held together in a plastic tube. The higher the sensitivity or *resolution* of the fiber-optic cable, the more glass fibers per bundle. High-resolution fiber-optic cables use approximately 25 to 50 glass filaments.

One benefit of having several lines in a fiber-optic cable is that a greater degree of flexibility is possible with the bundle. This narrow cable can be twisted and bent without any loss in the amount of light that is transmitted. Even colors can be carried through the fiber-optic cable. This light-transmission ability makes fiber-optic cable ideal for lighting areas that have limited or restricted access. In medicine, for example, a doctor can send a small fiber-optic cable through a vessel or cavity and light the area for viewing.

Further studies One of the hundreds of possible uses for fiber-optic systems is in data transmission. These data range from computer-generated data to telephone-produced voice information. A fiber-optic cable is able to carry these data without many of the problems that are commonly associated with wire-carried data. In fact, electrical interference is reduced with fiber-optic systems.

Can you design a simple experiment that would demonstrate a fiber-optic system's ability to carry data? (The device from Experiment 11 in part 1 might prove helpful in this experiment.)

Did you know? ○ When doctors use fiber optics, patients are able to recuperate faster because of the smaller incisions.

How do filters affect light?

Materials
- ❐ Prism
- ❐ Colored filters or colored cellophane in red, green, and blue
- ❐ White cardboard

Procedure
1. Use the prism to cast a visible spectrum of light on the white cardboard.
2. Hold a red filter in the spectrum between the prism and the white cardboard.
3. Hold a green filter in the spectrum between the prism and the white cardboard.
4. Hold a blue filter in the spectrum between the prism and the white cardboard.
5. Hold a red filter in the spectrum between the prism and the white cardboard. Then hold a green filter in the light passed by the red filter.
6. Observe all of the colors that pass through the various filter combinations and record your results.

Results You should have obtained the following results:

1. *Red filter* The red filter absorbs all colors of the visible spectrum except for red. Only red should be visible on the white cardboard.
2. *Green filter* The green filter absorbs all colors of the visible spectrum except for green. Only green should be visible on the white cardboard.
3. *Blue filter* The blue filter absorbs all colors of the visible spectrum except for blue. Only blue should be visible on the white cardboard.
4. *Red & green filters* The red filter absorbs all of the colors except

for red, while the green filter absorbs the red. No colors should be visible on the white cardboard.

Based on these observations, could you predict what various color filters will do to the visible spectrum? One useful application of this knowledge is in photography. Certain colored filters are placed on a camera's lens during black-and-white photography. These filters are used for darkening and lightening colors before the colors are recorded on the film. Predict what the results of this filter photography should be for various colors and colored-filter combinations. Were you correct?

Further studies Many filter absorptions can be difficult to observe. A better way to view them is with a spectroscope. To build a spectroscope, you will need (FIG. 39-1):

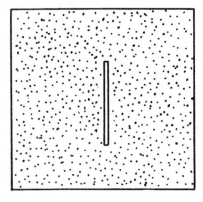

39-1 Plan for making a spectroscope viewer.

❒ Cardboard tube from an aluminum-foil roll
❒ 3-inch square of aluminum foil
❒ Knife
❒ Two rubber bands
❒ 3-inch square of diffraction grating

Use the rubber bands to hold the aluminum foil and the diffraction grating over opposite ends of the cardboard tube. With the knife, cut a 1-inch slit in the aluminum foil. Make sure that the edges of the slit are clean and straight.

Now, point the diffraction grating at an electric light source and look through the slit. You should see two visible light spectra. If you have difficulty seeing both of the spectra, rotate the aluminum foil cap until the two color bands are visible.

You can now repeat the color absorption experiment (above) using your spectroscope. Just hold the colored filters in front of the spectroscope as you view through the slit. Did you get the same results?

Did you know? ○ Filters are used on stage lights to create various "moods."

Experiment 40

How do sunglasses reduce glare?

Materials
- ❑ Two pair of Polaroid sunglasses
- ❑ Artificial light source

Procedure
1. Hold one pair of Polaroid sunglasses in each hand.
2. Place one lens from each pair of sunglasses on top of each other.
3. View the light source through this sunglasses-lens sandwich.
4. Slowly rotate one set of sunglasses.
5. Continue to observe the light source while rotating the sunglasses.

Results
Polaroid sunglasses are made from tourmaline crystals embedded in plastic, all having the same orientation. The tourmaline crystals form lines that are parallel to the ground. Rotating the two Polaroid lenses proved the existence of these parallel lines. When the lenses were perpendicular to each other, they blocked out all light.

In a pair of sunglasses, these lines serve to reduce the brightness of glare and reflections. *Glare* is produced by light waves reflecting on a shiny surface, such as snow, water, or glass. Light waves reflected off these surfaces follow erratic or scattered directions. As scattered light waves are reflected into these lenses, they are reduced by the tourmaline crystals. Finally, a tint in the lens also helps to minimize the brightness of the light.

Further studies
Polaroid lenses are also used in photography. A special polarizing filter can be fixed to the front of a camera lens. This filter is then rotated to place the grating at the best position for reducing glare.

Obtain a polarizing filter and experiment with photographs of glare. Does rotating the filter reduce the glare? An even greater degree of glare reduction is possible with two polarizing filters placed in series with each other. Put two polarizing filters on a camera and take some experimental photographs. What happens to the amount of light that reaches the film as the filters are rotated? Can too much rotation blank the lens? Why don't more photographers use this arrangement when taking pictures with glare?

How is a scale used for measuring weight?

Materials
- ❏ Unsharpened pencil
- ❏ Ball of string
- ❏ Two 2-x-2-inch thin cardboard sheets
- ❏ Five quarters
- ❏ Single-hole punch
- ❏ Scissors

Procedure
1. Punch four holes in the corners of each cardboard sheet.
2. Cut eight 3-inch pieces of string and tie one to each hole in the cardboard sheets.
3. Tie the four string pieces in each cardboard square into a common knot above the square.
4. Cut and attach a 12-inch piece of string to each knot.
5. Tie the two 12-inch strings to opposite ends of the pencil.
6. Find the center of gravity or balance point of the pencil with the two cardboard squares attached. To do this, hold the pencil so that the two cardboard squares hang down level and at equal heights.
7. Cut and tie a 6-inch length of string to the center of gravity of the pencil.
8. Your scale is now complete. The weight of the five quarters together equals (roughly) 1 ounce. By placing portions of this known weight on one cardboard square and an object of unknown weight on the other square, the weight of the unknown can be determined. How would you find the weight of the unknown by using this method?

Result
Your scale is more correctly known as a *balance* or a *beam scale*. This measurement device was originally developed in Egypt in approxi-

mately 5,000 B.C. There is very little difference in the operation of the Egyptian scale versus your scale. An object with an unknown weight is placed on one of the scale's weighing pans (this is the functional equivalent of your cardboard squares). This weight moves the one pan down and the other, empty pan up. Known weights are then placed on the open weighing pan. This lowers the higher weighing pan and raises the lower object pan. As more weights are added to the weighing pan, the object pan rises higher. Soon the two pans will be level. At this point, the weight of the object can be determined by adding together all of the weight on the weighing pan. This type of scale can be extremely accurate with small, lightweight objects.

Further studies   Before you will be able to make complete, accurate use of your scale, you will need to calibrate it. Calibration should allow you to measure objects that weigh as little as ¼ ounce. How would you calibrate your scale? You already have one fixed reference point for calibration-- five quarters is equal to 1 ounce. Based on this knowledge, how would you organize a set of weights that will measure ¼, ½, and ¾ ounce? The solution to this problem is to form an alternate set of weights. What would be a suitable weight standard? Once you have established a set of weights, what is the maximum weight that you can measure with your scale?

How do pulleys lift weights?

Materials
- ❒ Pulley
- ❒ Rope
- ❒ Cement block

Procedure

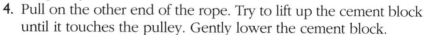

1. Firmly attach the pulley to a fixed beam. (This beam can be an existing arch or a beam you have constructed with several 2-x-4-inch pieces of wood.)
2. Run the rope directly over the pulley's wheel.
3. Tie the free end of the rope to the cement block. The rope tied to the cement block should be the free end that was run over the pulley's wheel.
4. Pull on the other end of the rope. Try to lift up the cement block until it touches the pulley. Gently lower the cement block.
5. Untie the rope from the cement block.
6. Untie the free end of the rope through a hole in the cement block.
7. Tie this end to the bottom hook on the pulley.
8. Once again, pull on the other end of the rope. Try to lift up the cement block until it touches the pulley. Lower the cement block carefully when you are finished.

Results A pulley is a simple machine. Simple machines multiply force or multiply distance or multiply speed. Pulleys multiply force by causing the force you apply to the pulley to travel through increased distances. The heavy object then is lifted but through a shorter distance.

There are two other uses for pulleys. First, a set of two pulleys can be used to alter the speed of a moving belt—a system found in the engine of most automobiles. In this type of system, one of the pulleys, the *driver*, is attached directly to the source of the movement. A steady rate of movement is supplied to the belt and the belt, in turn, moves the other pulley, which is usually a different size. This size difference results in either an increase in speed or an increase in power (*force*).

Another use for a pulley is in changing the direction of force. This example can be seen in your pulley experiment. In both pulley setups, you are pulling the rope in a direction that is opposite to the travel of the cement block. This directional force change does not always result in a speed change, but sometimes change in the direction of force is more important than the speed.

Further studies   To lift even heavier weights, you must use more than one pulley. This arrangement of multiple pulleys is called a *block and tackle* (FIG. 42-1). Various numbers of pulleys can yield an increased *mechanical advantage* (when the force needed to move an object is less than the weight of the object). For example, a two-pulley block and tackle has a mechanical advantage of two. Therefore, a 1-pound force will lift 2 pounds. Can you make a block and tackle with a mechanical advantage of four? How much force will be needed with this arrangement to lift a 200-pound weight?

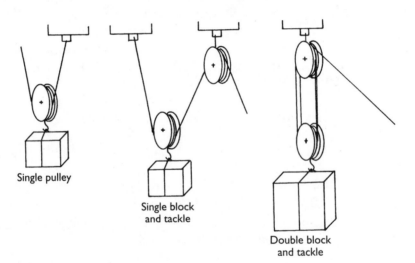

Single pulley

Single block and tackle

Double block and tackle

42-1   Three types of block and tackle.

Did you know?   ○ The fastest passenger-elevator lifts are in the "Sunshine 60" Building in Tokyo, Japan. Top speed is 22.72 miles per hour.

How do speakers work?

Materials
- ❐ Stereo speakers
- ❐ Tape recorder or turntable
- ❐ Prerecorded music (cassette tapes or records)
- ❐ Paper

Procedure
1. Set up your music system with a pair of stereo speakers attached to a tape recorder or a turntable.
2. Put some prerecorded music on your tape recorder or turntable.
3. Watch your speakers as the music is playing.
4. Hold a sheet of paper in front of each speaker. Watch and feel the sheet of paper while the music is playing.

Results
As a speaker vibrates, it moves the surrounding air. This air movement mimics the speaker movement. The surrounding air movement produces waves of sound. These sound waves are called *compressional waves*. In your stereo system, sound is not traveling through the wires between your turntable and the speakers. Instead, the wire is carrying changes in electrical voltages that cause the magnets in your speakers to move or vibrate the speaker's cone. The movement of the cone produces compression waves that travel through the surrounding air as sound waves. When these sound waves reach the ear, they are converted into sound.

Further studies
Sound and the physics of acoustics present many different sources for additional experimentation. You can actually "see" the waves produced by sound through two experiments. One experiment requires an *oscilloscope*, a scientific test instrument that displays wave patterns on a *cathode ray tube* (CRT). Just connect a microphone to an oscilloscope and observe the wave patterns from different sounds.

Other sound experiments are much easier to do in your laboratory.

Materials   ❒ Tuning fork
         ❒ Flat bowl
         ❒ Water

Procedure   1. Fill the dish with water.
         2. Strike the tuning fork.
         3. While the fork is still vibrating, touch the surface of the water.
         4. A violent wave will be produced in the water. This wave might physically splash the water.

You can perform many exotic experiments with sound. In this case, objects can be made to vibrate from the vibrations of another vibrating object. This effect is called *sympathetic vibration*. Can you create an experiment that would demonstrate sympathetic vibration?

Other interesting sound experiments could investigate the Doppler effect. The *Doppler effect* is the sudden change in pitch that is heard from moving objects. How would you prove the existence of the Doppler effect?

Did you know?   ◯ Speakers can be used as microphones in many electrical sound systems.

Appendix

Suppliers, Services, & Software

Supplies CAROLINA BIOLOGICAL SUPPLY COMPANY
Burlington, NC 27215
(919) 584-0381

The leading supplier of scientific materials for schools and other educational institutions is Carolina Biological Supply Company. Living, as well as preserved, specimens can be purchased from the company, which also offers an excellent selection of scientific equipment for research in every scientific discipline.

CHILDCRAFT EDUCATION CORPORATION
20 Kilmer Road
Edison, NJ 08818
(809) 631-5657

Educational toys and other goodies fill the pages of Childcraft's 47-page color catalog. Among the many items of educational merit are several of scientific interest. Most of the products sold by Childcraft Education Corporation are for youngsters under 13 years of age.

EDMUND SCIENTIFIC COMPANY
101 E. Gloucester Pike
Barrington, NJ 08007

Edmund Scientific Company started as a scientific surplus equipment dealer. This business quickly mushroomed into a general-purpose science "thing" dealer. You can purchase virtually any exotic scientific tool that you will ever need or want from this company. From lasers to giant 8-inch reflecting telescopes, Edmund Scientific Company has it all.

GULF COAST RESEARCH LABORATORY
P.O. Box AG
Ocean Springs, MS 39564

Gulf Coast Research Laboratory is an educational institution that prints a marvelous set of informational leaflets. Each of these leaflets discusses a separate marine biology topic. The information is accurate, and the leaflets are free (check with the firm for a change in this policy).

HEATH COMPANY
Benton Harbor, MI 49022

Heath Company's chief claim to fame is its offering of high-quality electronic construction kits. These are the finest kits you will find anywhere on the market. These kits range from easy-to-construct radio projects to complex digital computers. Each kit comes complete with all of the parts necessary to build the project. Additionally, a detailed set of assembly instructions will guide you through the construction process.

JDR MICRODEVICES
1224 S. Bascom Avenue
San Jose, CA 95128
(800) 538-5000

JDR Microdevices is an electronics parts supplier. Its prices are reasonable and its service is prompt. If you have any trouble locating the parts needed for any of the electronics experiments in this book, call JDR Microdevices.

RADIO SHACK
(Local stores)

Many of the major electronic parts in this book have been referenced with Radio Shack catalog part numbers to enable you to purchase the bulk of your construction materials in your local store. If your local Radio Shack is out of a particular part, it can be ordered. An average order will arrive in less than one week.

Services   Hundreds of services are available to the young scientist for providing assistance in pursuing scientific research. Memberships, information, and support can be obtained from these scientific societies, zoological parks, and information agencies. Please contact the service that will best satisfy your scientific research requirements and consult with their staff about your intended experiment.

Societies   NATIONAL AUDUBON SOCIETY
950 Third Avenue
New York, NY 10022

NATIONAL WILDLIFE FEDERATION
1412 16th Street, N.W.
Washington, D.C. 20036

WORLD WILDLIFE FUND
1255 23rd Street, N.W.
Washington, D.C. 20037

Zoological parks   AUDUBON ZOOLOGICAL GARDEN
6500 Magazine Street
New Orleans, LA

CENTRAL PARK ZOO
5th Avenue and 64th Street
New York, NY

LINCOLN PARK ZOOLOGICAL Gardens
Stockton Drive at Fullerton Avenue
Chicago, IL

LOS ANGELES ZOO
5333 Zoo Drive
Los Angeles, CA

NATIONAL ZOO
National Zoological Park
Washington, D.C.

Information
agencies   ART, SCIENCE & TECHNOLOGY INSTITUTE
Dupont Circle Metro
2018 R Street, N.W.
Washington, D.C.

ASTRONOMY PROGRAM
University of Maryland
College Park, MD 20742

DEPARTMENT OF ENTOMOLOGY
New Mexico State University
Las Cruces, NM 88003

FLORIDA STATE COLLECTION OF ARTHROPODS
Division of Plant Industry
P.O. Box 1269
Gainesville, FL 32602

GODDARD INSTITUTE FOR SPACE STUDIES
2880 Broadway
New York, NY 10025

JET PROPULSION LABORATORY
4800 Oak Grove Drive
Pasadena, CA 91109

NATIONAL SPACE SCIENCE DATA CENTER
Goddard Flight Center
Greenbelt, MD 20771

NEW YORK PUBLIC LIBRARY
5th Avenue and 42nd Street
New York, NY 10018

PHILADELPHIA ACADEMY OF NATURAL SCIENCES
19th Street and Benjamin Franklin Parkway
Philadelphia, PA 19102

SMITHSONIAN NATIONAL MUSEUMS

Smithsonian Institution Building
Anacostia Museum
Arthur M. Sackler Gallery
Arts and Industries Building
Enid A. Haupt Garden
Frer Gallery of Art
Hirshhorn Museum and Sculpture Garden
International Gallery
National Air and Space Museum
National Museum of African Art
National Museum of American Art
National Museum of American History
National Museum of Natural History
National Portrait Gallery
National Zoological Park

Renwick Gallery
National Gallery of Art
Washington, D.C. 20560

U.S. PATENT AND TRADEMARK OFFICES
Washington, D.C. 20231

U.S. GEOLOGICAL SURVEY
National Center
Reston, VA 22092

Software AUTODESK, INC.
2320 Marinship Way
Sausalito, CA 94965

AutoCAD Release 11

This is the premier computer-aided design (CAD) drafting program. AutoCAD is capable of matching the features and performance of large dedicated CAD workstations, but costs thousands of dollars less. In fact, AutoCAD is the only personal computer CAD software that is able to satisfy the rigid demands of professional engineering design work without mandating the purchase of specialized computer equipment. Remarkably, even with such a powerful product, Autodesk has managed to minimize the need for complex commands.

ELECTRONIC ARTS
1450 Fashion Island Blvd.
San Mateo, CA 94404

Armor Alley

Armor Alley pits one opponent against another of equal strength and ability. Each player attempts to eliminate the other from the battlefield by destroying all of their helicopters or their home base.

The Blue Max

A historical flying simulation set over France during 1917. Eight different aircraft and seven missions are available to the prospective pilot.

Das Boot

Based on the actual accounts of German U-Boat captain, Peter Ali Cremer, one of the three surviving U-Boat captains in 1945. Spectacular 3-D viewing angles guide the player in manning seven U-Boat stations.

Chuck Yeager's Air Combat

General Chuck Yeager serves as the omnipresent copilot, giving instructions and advice before and after combat missions and even during intense mid-air dogfights. Over 50 actual historic missions can be chosen by the player and flown from either side.

Harpoon

This popular naval simulation has been updated to follow events in the Mediterranean Sea and its smaller interconnected waters.

Mario Andretti's Racing Challenge

Players progress through six professional racing circuits following Mario Andretti's career. Players are put in the driver's seat of six high-performance racing machines.

MegaFortress

This simulation is based on the nationally acclaimed best-selling novel *Flight of the Old Dog*. A fully renovated, "super" B-52 bomber with all of the latest in weapons and avionics high technology and its ensuing missions is portrayed with stunning 256 color three-dimensional graphics.

Overrun!

Overrun! is a modern land warfare simulation where Europe and the Middle East serve as near-future battlefields. Set in 1992, Overrun! includes helicopters and new and near-future weapon systems.

Second Front

This is a division-level strategic game on a scale that will appeal to advanced war-gamers. The map extends from Berlin in the west to Stalingrad in the east, and covers the entire Russian Front.

Secret Weapons of the Luftwaffe

This could be the most advanced World War II air combat simulator for personal computers. The software recreates one of the longest and most fascinating air offenses in history dealing with the campaign by the U. S. Eighth Air Force against Germany from 1943 to 1945.

Typhoon of Steel

Players compete in three theaters: Pacific Theater, Asian Theater, and European Theater involving American troops versus German troops.

GENERIC SOFTWARE
11911 North Creek Parkway South
Bothell, WA 98011

Generic 3D

Generic 3D is a CAD program that is capable of taking the would-be architect, engineer, or designer to the highest level of drafting excellence without the labor of a complex array of commands. A unique color-coded cursor, tracking, and 3-D coordinate system expertly guide the user to the exact point that requires the drafter's touch. Once you've found the right spot, floating-point precision and elaborate zoom commands enlarge the screen for accurate drafting. Shading and lighting can be added to any design through two-letter commands and simple mouse-strokes. When you've completed your design several forms of output can be generated. Color monitors, printers, and plotters are more than capable of turning Generic 3D's output into detailed engineering plans.

MICROPROSE
180 Lakefront Drive
Hunt Valley, MD 21030

Civilization

This simulation begins in 4000 B.C., and the player must develop an entire civilization from a small, nomadic tribe. As the tribe grows, smaller groups can seek new people, territory, and trade. The result is to survive into the future year 2000 A.D.

Command HQ

Players compete in World War I, World War II, or even World War III. Each player determines strategy, moves armies, navies, and air power to conquer territories, acquire resources, and assimilate nations. When a particular battle commences, all of the action is seen through detailed animation that appears on the computer's screen.

F-117A Stealth Fighter

Recognized internationally for its realistic military simulations, MicroProse Software, Inc. has mastered new technological advances that make their products leaders in the software industry. In this simulation, players fly in nine world areas against exciting missions. The enemy in each mission is based on artificial intelligence software that is capable of matching the player's moves with similar computer-generated actions (FIG. A-1).

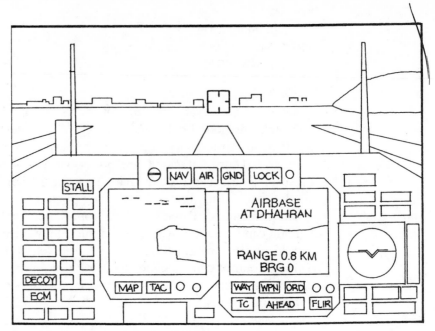

A-1 View out the cockpit of an F-117A.

Knights of the Sky

Each player assumes the role of a World War I American, British, or French aviator. Players navigate with authentic maps and simulated compass headings and chart their location by observing realistic roads, rivers, and other ground landmarks. This feature makes the player act in a manner similar to the actions of real World War I pilots. A unique playing aspect of this game allows two pilots to "fly" into combat against each other via a modem link between two computers. Therefore, pilots could dogfight with each other hundreds of miles apart over the telephone lines and a modem.

Universal Military Simulator II

Historical battles can be simulated and fought exactly as they were fought or with player-designed modifications. The introduction of these modifications allows battles between Robert E. Lee and Napoleon to be fought out on the personal computer. The scope of this software is global and encompasses 127 nations, 525 provinces, and 32,000 military units. Players can control which armies are fighting, the size, strength, and morale of those armies and the terrain on which they fight. Each battle is depicted on a unique 3-D grid system that allows the player to view the battles from any angle. A UMS II Planet Editor can be used to design entirely new worlds with oceans, mountain ranges, and land masses.

Glossary

absorbency the capacity to absorb or take up.

acid a compound that reacts with a base to form a salt and is capable of turning blue litmus paper red.

acoustics relating to the science of sound, dealing with its production, transmission, and reception.

aerobatics aerial maneuvers performed by an aircraft.

aerodynamics the science dealing with air motions and its effect on airborne bodies.

agar a culture medium that is derived from red algae.

ailerons an aircraft's control surface that governs roll.

airfoil a design structure that generates a desired motion effect when it is introduced into an airflow. Airfoils can be found on wings, as well as aircraft propellers.

algae any of a group of single-celled aquatic plants.

amplifier a device for increasing or amplifying a circuit's power or current.

analog in computers, a device that assigns mechanical changes in voltage or movement to numbers.

anatomy a science that deals with the physical structure of organisms.

Anaximander credited with being the first biologist, 610–547 B.C., although he is more widely known as a philosopher and astronomer.

Aristotle a Greek philosopher and zoologist in 384–322 B.C.

astronomy a science that studies the movements, compositions, and influences of celestial bodies

atomic structure the representation of a chemical element in terms of the number of protons in its nucleus along with any orbiting electrons.

Bardeen, John   an American physicist born in 1908; contributed to the development of the transistor.

barometric pressure   the pressure of the atmosphere.

base   a compound that reacts with an acid to form a salt and will turn red litmus paper blue.

BASIC   an acronym for a computer programming language that means Beginner's All-purpose Symbolic Instruction Code.

Beaufort, Sir Francis   a British admiral in 1774–1857 who designed the Beaufort wind scale.

Beaufort wind scale   a scale that is used to indicate the force of a wind. The velocity of the winds that are measured on this scale range from 0–136 mph.

Bernoulli, Jacques   a Swiss mathematician born in 1705.

binary number system   a base-two number system that uses combinations of 0 and 1 for representing other numbers.

biochemistry   a science that studies the chemical compounds and processes that happen in organisms.

biology   a science that studies the processes of organisms.

biplanes   two-winged aircraft.

black hole   a theoretical area of outer space that resulted from the collapse of a star.

block and tackle   a combination of pulleys and ropes that are used for lifting or hoisting a weight.

botany   a science that studies the structure and processes of plants.

Brattain, Walter Houser   an American physicist born in 1902 who contributed to the design of the transistor.

Bréquet, Louis and Jacques   French aviation-pioneer brothers who flew the first helicopter in 1907.

buttress   a stone, masonry, or wood structure that supports a wall or a building.

chemistry   the science studying the structure, reactions, and properties of elements, molecules, ions, and compounds.

chips   a slang term for integrated circuits.

chromatography   a technique for separating a compound into discrete solutes that represent its various components.

comets   an orbiting celestial body with a bright center and a variously elongated tail.

compression   a process for compacting or squeezing into a reduced volume.

compressional waves   a longitudinal wave. A sound wave is an example.

concave lens a lens that is rounded inward.

condensation the reduction of matter into a denser form.

conductivity the conducting or transmission of energy.

conservation the retention of an amount during a reaction.

constellation an arrangement or configuration of stars that has been mapped into an accepted pattern. There are 88 officially recognized constellations in the night sky.

convex lens a lens that is rounded outward.

crystallization the process of forming crystals.

da Vinci, Leonardo an Italian painter and engineer from 1452–1519.

Darwin, Charles an English naturalist from 1809–1882.

De Forest, Lee an American inventor living in 1873–1961.

decay to decrease or decline in quantity or force.

Democritus a Greek philosopher living in 400 B.C.

dew point the temperature when water vapor begins to condense.

Doppler effect a change in wave frequency that increases or decreases with relation to the speed and distance between the wave's source and its destination.

drag a force limiting the movement of an aircraft through the air.

eclipse the total or partial obscuring of one celestial object by another one.

ecology the study of the interrelationship between organisms and their environment.

Edison, Thomas A. an American inventor who lived from 1847–1931.

Einstein, Albert the German physicist from 1879–1955.

electrode a material made into a conductor for forming an electrical contact.

electrolyte a nonmetallic material made into a conductor through ionic movement.

electromagnetism magnetism generated by electrical current.

electromagnet a material that is surrounded by wire and charged with electrical current forming a magnetic core.

emulsion a liquid suspension.

erosion to diminish or destroy a substance through a slow and methodical application of a reducing agent.

evaporation to deposit or dissipate into a vapor.

expansion to enlarge or increase the size or capacity of function.

Faraday, Michael the English chemist living from 1791–1867.

fossils an organism or other organic matter preserved in a mineralized or petrified condition.

friction a force that generates resistance between two objects that are in motion.

Galileo an Italian astronomer from 1564–1642. Galileo's real name was Galilei.

genetics a science that studies the developmental variation and heredity of an organism.

geotropism a growth factor in plants that is affected by gravity.

gnomon a shadow indicator on a sundial.

humidity moisture in the atmosphere.

Huygens, Christian a Dutch mathematician born in 1629.

hybridization the production of hybrids through selective interbreeding.

infrared light light that is outside the visible spectrum.

integrated circuits complex electronic functions that are reduced onto single silicon wafers.

ionization the partial or total conversion of matter into ions.

keystone the wedge-shaped piece at the top of an arch. The keystone is used to keep that arch from collapsing.

latitude a line of angular distance around the earth between the north and south poles.

Leeuwenhoek, Anton a Dutch naturalist from 1632–1723.

lift a force on an airfoil that raises the aircraft up and counteracts the force of gravity.

Linnaeus, Carolus a Swedish botanist from 1707–1778.

litmus paper a paper that has been treated with litmus. Litmus is a coloring material that is derived from lichens.

logarithms an exponent that represents a number's power for equaling a given number.

magnification an enlargement factor.

Maxwell, James C. a Scottish physicist from 1831–1879.

Mendel, Gregor Johann the Austrian botanist born in 1822.

metamorphosis a process for changing in physical form as part of a developmental cycle.

meteorology   the science of weather and weather forecasting.

microbiology   the science of microorganisms.

Montgolfier, J.E. and J. M.   the French ballooning brothers born in the mid 1700s.

Morse, Samuel   the American inventor born in 1791.

NASA   National Aeronautics and Space Administration.

Newton, Sir Isaac   an English mathematician from 1642–1727.

nova   a star that increases its light output and then fades away.

oscillation   a periodic change or fluctuation in electricity flow.

oxidation   a process of combining a compound with oxygen.

Pavlov, Ivan   a Russian physiologist from 1849–1936.

pH   a representation of the hydrogen-ion concentration that indicates acidity and alkalinity in terms of a negative logarithm.

photosynthesis   the production of carbohydrates through chlorophyll reacting with light energy.

physiology   a science that studies the functions of organisms.

pigmentation   coloration with pigments.

pitch   the up and down movement of an aircraft as controlled by the horizontal stabilizer.

radiation   the expulsion of energy in waves.

Ramsay, William   a British chemist from 1852–1916.

reflection   the mirror or production of light or sound waves from a surface.

refraction   the deflection of a light or sound wave through a material.

relative humidity   the ratio of the amount of water vapor in the atmosphere to the amount of vapor that the atmosphere can hold.

respiration   the processes of supplying oxygen to an organism's cells.

Roentgen   the German physicist from 1845–1923.

semiconductors   a silicon (or other element) wafer that varies its electrical potential according to temperature.   Semiconductors are used in the preparation of integrated circuits.

Shockley, William   an American physicist born in 1910.

spectra   the plural of spectrum. An accumulation of wave emissions.

springer   the stone that is at the base of an arch against the impost.

Sullivan, Louis   the American architect from 1856–1924.

superconductivity the loss of electrical resistance as a factor of low temperature.

supernova the explosion of a star.

supersaturated solution a solution that contains more material than it is capable of normally holding.

surface tension the surface of a fluid that forms an elastic skin.

Theophrastus the Greek naturalist from 300 B.C.

thrust a force the reacts against drag and moves a body forward like an aircraft.

Torricelli, Evangelista Italian mathematician from 1608–1647.

tractor a pulling force.

triodes an electron tube with three parts: anode, cathode, and control grid.

turbulence irregular currents in a fluid medium like water or air.

vibration the movement of particles in equal and opposite directions.

voussoirs the wedge pieces forming the body of an arch.

waning moon a moon that is reducing in size and intensity.

waxing moon a moon that is increasing in size and intensity.

Wright, Orville and Wilbur the American aviation pioneer brothers born in the late 1800s.

X rays a short wavelength radiation that is capable of penetrating thick solids.

yaw movement about a vertical axis (left to right) in an aircraft.

zoology a science that studies animals.

Index